THE
EVERYTHING KIDS'®
Cookbook

From mac 'n cheese to double chocolate chip cookies—
all you need to have some finger lickin' fun

Sandra K. Nissenberg, M.S., R.D.

Adams Media Corporation
Avon, Massachusetts

EDITORIAL
Publishing Director: Gary M. Krebs
Managing Editor: Kate McBride
Copy Chief: Laura MacLaughlin
Acquisitions Editor: Cheryl Kimball
Development Editor: Christel A. Shea

PRODUCTION
Production Director: Susan Beale
Production Manager: Michelle Roy Kelly
Series Designer: Colleen Cunningham
Layout and Graphics: Brooke Camfield,
Colleen Cunningham, Rachael Eiben,
Michelle Roy Kelly, Daria Perreault

Published by Adams Media, an F+W Publications Company
57 Littlefield Street, Avon, MA 02322 USA
www.adamsmedia.com

ISBN 10: 1-58062-658-0
ISBN 13: 978-1-58062-658-3
Printed in the United States of America.

J I H

Library of Congress Cataloging-in-Publication Data
Nissenberg, Sandra K.
The everything kids' cookbook / Sandra K. Nissenberg.
p.   cm.   —(An everything series book)
Summary: Information on cooking terms, measuring, kitchen safety, and nutrition precedes recipes for all sorts of dishes for breakfast, lunch, dinner, dessert, and snacks.
ISBN 1-58062-658-0
1. Cookery—Juvenile literature. [1. Cookery.] I. Title. II.
Everything series.
TX652.5 .N57 2002
641.5'123—dc21
2002008607

Cover illustrations by Dana Regan.
Interior illustrations by Kurt Dolber and Eulala Connor.
Puzzles by Beth Blair.

Puzzle Power Software by Centron Software Technologies, Inc. was used to create puzzle grids.

*This book is available at quantity discounts for bulk purchases.
For information, call 1-800-289-0963.*

See the entire Everything® series at *everything.com*.

Contents

Introduction

It's a fact: You are an interesting person. You like to do things your way, especially when it comes to picking out foods to eat. Some people love to eat, and will try anything and everything. Others only want the same foods, day after day. And still others would choose only a few different things if their parents would allow it.

When it comes to cooking, though, a lot of kids might be the same. Cooking is a chance to make a mess (okay, and clean it up, too) . . . it's a chance to play and experiment with foods . . . and most important, it's a chance to share creations and concoctions with friends and families. Sometimes, especially if you haven't spent a lot of time watching the cooks in your house, you might need a little help along the way.

The Everything® Kids' Cookbook is a book to help you get started. You will learn your way around the kitchen, and get to choose your own favorites from the many tasty recipes in the next pages. You will learn about food and cooking, too! This book includes information on safety tips, basic cooking tools and terms, and healthy eating to help all cooks from beginners to masters.

This book hasn't forgotten the fun, either! Along the way, you'll find games, puzzles, and fun food trivia scattered throughout the pages.

You (and adults, too!) will get great ideas and useful knowledge and information from *The Everything® Kids' Cookbook*. When it comes to having fun in the kitchen, everyone is a kid who can enjoy making fun, delicious creations with their families while building memories that will last a lifetime.

Happy, healthy eating for you and your family,

While cooking, children must be supervised by a responsible adult at all times.

Chapter 1

Let's Get Cooking

Tasty Tuna Melt

Tuna melts make a great lunch, or you can share them as an afternoon snack.

▶ Difficulty: Medium

Makes 4 tuna melt sandwich halves

2 English muffins or bagels, split in half
1 6-ounce can chunk tuna, canned in water, drained
2 Tbsp. mayonnaise
¼ cup shredded or sliced cheese: cheddar, mozzarella, or American

1. Preheat the oven, or toaster oven, to 350 degrees.
2. Place English muffin or bagel halves onto a cookie sheet or a sheet of aluminum foil.
3. Use the can opener to open the tuna, then carefully drain the water out.
4. In a small bowl, combine the drained tuna with the mayonnaise. Mix well.
5. Top each English muffin or bagel half with tuna, then with the shredded or sliced cheese.
6. Bake 5–8 minutes, or until the cheese is melted.

The best things about cooking are that you can be creative, experiment, and share what you make. Like any activity that involves experiments, there are tools, and terms, and things to know so the only surprise in your kitchen is how easy cooking can be.

The next few sections aren't as exciting as making Mini-Pizzas (page 39) or Banana Split Ice Cream Pie (page 98), but they are pretty important. Otherwise, how will you know whether to bake or boil? Slice or mash?

Read this chapter with your parents, or the adult that will be helping you in the kitchen. The recipes are written for you, but it's important for *all* the cooks to know what's going on.

Reading Recipes

Recipes are a set of instructions for making a particular food. It is important to read the recipe thoroughly so you understand how to make the food and what ingredients you will need to make it. A typical recipe should include the following:

- Level of difficulty
- Tools of the trade
- Quantity (or number of servings) that the recipe makes
- An ingredient list
- Oven temperature (if necessary)
- Easy-to-understand instructions
- Baking or cooking times

Important Safety Tips and Kitchen Rules

Safety should be your *number one* priority when working and cooking in the kitchen. Hot food or pans, boiling water, and sharp knives all can be dangerous if you don't know how to handle them properly. Always check with an adult or parent before working in the kitchen, and be sure to review these handy safety tips and kitchen rules before starting:

- *Be sure to wash your hands with soap and water before touching food.* It is also important to wash your hands after handling raw meat or fish, before you start touching other things.
- *Tie back long hair and pull up long sleeves.* First, you want to keep them out of your food. Second, for safety reasons you need to keep long or loose things away from things like blenders or the flame on your stove.
- *Read the entire recipe before you begin.* Find out what ingredients and utensils you will need. You'll also want to know how long a recipe takes to prepare, and how many people it will feed.
- *Make a shopping list of things you need.* Include items you will need to keep the kitchen well stocked (such as sugar, eggs, or milk).
- *Start with a clean cooking area.* Otherwise, dirty dishes will be in your way, dirty counters will ruin your food, and other things on the counter or table (like mail) may get stained or splashed while you cook.
- *Don't overfill pots and pans.* If they overflow while you are cooking, you will definitely end up with a mess, and you might get splattered or splashed with hot liquids.
- *Know how to use the various appliances and utensils you will need.* If you need to, ask an adult to teach or remind you, especially if you are using anything with hot oil (like a wok), or sharp moving parts (like a food processor).
- *Be careful with knives.* Learn how to hold them, wash them, and store them properly.
- *Put ingredients away when you have finished with them.* Also, be sure to turn off all appliances when you're done.
- *Wipe counters clean while working.* Put dirty dishes in the sink to keep them away from the clean ones.
- *Keep electric appliances away from water or the sink.* Also, try to keep the cords up on the counter so you don't trip or step on them by accident.
- *Always use potholders or oven mitts to touch hot pans and dishes.* You may not realize how hot something is until you've picked it up, so it's always better to start out with your hands protected.
- *Know where to find things, and where to put them away.* By keeping everything in its place, you will have a clean cooking area, and you won't lose things.
- *Do only one job at a time.* Cooking requires planning and concentration—it's a lot like juggling! As you practice, you can do more and more, but in the beginning, just focus on one thing.

Adults should supervise all your food preparation and cooking activities. It's important for you to learn how to work in a kitchen—and enjoy it!—but it's also important that you remember safety. Make sure an adult knows exactly what you are doing, and will be able to give help if you need it.

The recipes in this book list the tools in advance, so you know if you have everything you will need. The information about difficulty is pretty helpful for you, too, so you know if you'll need an adult around. Some recipes can go from HARD to EASY just by having an adult do the cutting with sharp knives—it's that easy!

Tools of the Trade

Proper tools are a must for preparing food. Let's take a look at some of the most common cooking utensils and equipment you can find in the kitchen . . .

 Baking pan—a square or rectangular pan (glass or metal) used for baking and cooking food in the oven

 Blender—an electric appliance used for blending liquids and grinding food

 Can opener—a tool, either manual or electric, designed to open cans

 Casserole dish—a glass dish, usually a 1-quart or 2-quart size, used to make casseroles or baked goods in the oven

 Colander—a metal (or sometimes plastic) bowl with holes in it used to drain water or liquid from foods (such as pasta or vegetables)

 Cookie sheet—a flat metal sheet used for baking cookies or other non-runny items

 Cutting board—a board made from wood or hard plastic used when cutting or chopping ingredients

 Electric mixer—an electric appliance used for mixing ingredients (like cake batter) together

 Glass measuring cup—a glass cup, used to measure liquids, with various measurements printed along the side

 Ice cream scoop—a plastic or metal tool, shaped like a giant spoon, used to scoop ice cream from a carton

 Measuring cups—plastic or metal cups in different sizes, used to measure dry ingredients

 Measuring spoons—plastic or metal spoons in different sizes, used to measure smaller amounts of both liquid and dry ingredients

 Meat mallet—a tool used to pound, flatten, and tenderize beef, chicken, and other meat

Microwave oven—a small oven that cooks food very quickly by cooking with electromagnetic waves (microwaves)

 Mixing bowls—bowls (in various sizes) in which you mix ingredients together

 Muffin tins—metal or glass pans with small, round cups used for baking muffins and cupcakes

 Oven—a kitchen appliance for baking or broiling food

 Oven mitts/pot holders—mittens or pads used to hold hot pots, pans, baking sheets, and plates

 Pastry brush—a small brush used to spread melted butter or margarine, or sauces over food

 Pizza cutter—a tool with a rolling cutter used to easily cut pizzas, dough, or breads

 Plate—a flat dish used to serve food

 Potato masher—a tool used to mash cooked potatoes, or anything soft, to make them smooth

 Rolling pin—a wooden or plastic roller used to flatten an item such as dough for a piecrust

 Saucepan—a pot with a projecting handle used for stovetop cooking

 Skillet—a pan used for frying, stir-frying, and sautéing food in hot fat or oil

 Spatula—a flat metal or plastic utensil used to lift, turn, and flip foods like eggs, cookies, and hamburgers

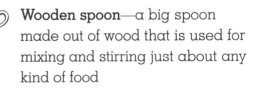 **Stove**—a kitchen appliance with gas or electric burners used for cooking food (also called "range")

Vegetable peeler—sometimes called a potato or carrot peeler, used to peel the skin off of fruit or vegetables

 Whisk—a utensil used for mixing and stirring liquid ingredients, like eggs and milk, together

 Wooden spoon—a big spoon made out of wood that is used for mixing and stirring just about any kind of food

Things to Know Before You Begin

It can sometimes be confusing to understand all the words for different ways to prepare and cook foods in a recipe. Here is a reference guide to help.

Bake—to cook something inside the oven, using the heat from the bottom

Batter—a mixture made from ingredients like sugar, eggs, flour, and water that is used to make cakes, cookies, and pancakes

Beat—to mix hard with a spoon, fork, whisk, or electric mixer

Blend—to mix foods together until smooth

Boil—to cook in a liquid until bubbles appear or until a liquid reaches its boiling point (water boils at 212 degrees Fahrenheit/100 degrees Celsius). Note: Water cannot get hotter than its boiling point, it can only make steam faster.

Broil—to put food under the broiler part of the oven, where the heat source is on top of the food

Brown—to cook at low to medium heat until foods turn brown

Chill—to refrigerate food until it is cold

Chop—to cut food into small pieces with a knife, blender, or food processor

Cool—to let the food sit at room temperature until it is no longer hot

Cream—to mix ingredients like sugar, butter, and eggs together until they are smooth and creamy

Dice—to chop food into small, square (like dice), even-sized pieces

Drain—to pour off a liquid in which the food has been cooked or stored

Drizzle—to sprinkle drops of liquid, like chocolate syrup or an icing, lightly over the top of something like cookies, or a cake

Fold—to gently combine ingredients together from top to bottom until they are just mixed together

Figure 1-1 Common cooking methods

Bake

Boil

Simmer

Stir-Fry

Grate—to shred food into tiny pieces with a shredder, blender, or food processor

Grease—to rub a baking pan or a dish with butter, margarine, or oil so food cooked on it won't stick (Canned cooking spray will work, too.)

Knead—to fold, press, and turn dough to make it the right consistency

Mince—to cut food into very small pieces

Mix—to stir two or more ingredients together until they are evenly combined

Preheat—to turn the oven on to the desired temperature and let it heat up before using it for cooking

Puree—to mix in a blender or food processor until food is smooth and has the consistency of applesauce or a milkshake

Sauté—to cook food on the stovetop in a skillet with a little liquid or oil

Simmer—to cook over low heat until the food almost boils

Slice—to cut food into even-sized pieces

Stir—to continuously mix food with a spoon

Stir-fry—to cook food on the stovetop in a very hot pan while stirring constantly

Steam—to put food over a pan of boiling water so the steam can cook it

Whip—to beat rapidly with a whisk, electric mixer, or an eggbeater

Bubbles

In each of the circles is the name of a favorite fun food—minus one letter! Figure out the missing letter to finish the word. Then arrange the missing letters to spell the name of a bonus fun food.

1. A F E L W

2. I D P N G

3. L O E S N O

4. R T G I E O L

5. I F S R

1. _____

2. _____

3. _____

4. _____

5. _____

BONUS: _____

Measuring Ingredients

To make a recipe properly, it is necessary to measure ingredients accurately. Your cooking tools should include measuring spoons and a set of measuring cups for both liquid and dry measurements.

Glass measuring cups are used to measure liquids like milk and water. These cups are marked with different measurements (¼ cup, ⅓ cup, ½ cup, ⅔ cup, ¾ cup, and 1 cup) so you can see how high to fill them.

Stacked measuring cups for dry ingredients come in specific sizes. The sets are usually made from either plastic or metal, and there are separate cups for each measurement. You usually use these cups for dry ingredients, like flour and sugar.

Measuring spoons measure small amounts of either liquid or dry ingredients.

Unless the recipe says to use a "rounded" measure, make sure to fill the cup or spoon evenly to the top. Level off dry ingredients using a blunt knife or spatula. Soft ingredients, like brown sugar, peanut butter, or shortening, get packed in, as shown in Figure 1-2.

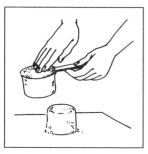
Measuring Brown Sugar

Measuring Soft Ingredients

Measuring Liquid

Measuring Dry Ingredients

Measuring Butter

Using Measuring Spoon

Figure 1-2 Measuring methods: Some ingredients are measured differently from others. These diagrams will help you.

Common Cooking Abbreviations and Equivalent Measures

Most recipes use abbreviations for the measurements of your ingredients. Here is a quick guide to know what standard abbreviations mean:

It is also helpful to know what different measurements equal. This quick reference will give you the basics:

Common Abbreviations

ABBREVIATION		MEASUREMENT
t. or tsp.	=	teaspoon
T. or Tbsp.	=	tablespoon
c.	=	cup
pt.	=	pint
qt.	=	quart
oz.	=	ounce
lb.	=	pound
pkg.	=	package

Figure 1-3 How Much Is "a Little"?

RECIPE MEASUREMENT		WHAT IT EQUALS (EQUIVALENT)
a pinch/dash	=	less than ⅛ teaspoon
3 teaspoons	=	1 tablespoon
¼ cup	=	4 tablespoons
⅓ cup	=	5 tablespoons + 1 teaspoon
½ cup	=	8 tablespoons
⅔ cup	=	10 tablespoons + 2 teaspoons
½ pint	=	1 cup
1 cup (dry ingredients)	=	16 tablespoons
1 cup (liquid)	=	8 ounces
2 cups (liquid)	=	1 pint or ½ quart
4 cups (liquid)	=	1 quart
4 quarts (liquid)	=	1 gallon
8 ounces	=	½ pound
16 ounces	=	2 pints or ½ quart liquid
16 ounces	=	1 pound
32 ounces	=	1 quart
64 ounces	=	½ gallon
1 liter	=	1.06 quarts
1 quart	=	.95 liter

Measuring Spoon Math

Margarita is baking a cake. The recipe calls for:
  2 cups flour
  1½ cups sugar
  ¼ cup cocoa
Unfortunately, Margarita only has a tablespoon with which to measure. Do you know how many tablespoons (Tbsp.) she will need of each ingredient? HINT: 1 cup = 16 Tbsp.

Flour = _____ Tbsp.

Sugar = _____ Tbsp.

Cocoa = _____ Tbsp.

Nutrition to Know

Have you ever wondered *why* we eat? Or *what* we eat? We eat to keep nourished . . . to stay alive. Just like a car needs gasoline, people need fuel, and food keeps us moving. Without it we could not survive.

Nutrients

Every food we eat has substances in it called nutrients. When we talk about nutrition, we are talking about these nutrients, all the substances that are in our food. There are over fifty different nutrients—some you have

Play It Safe

When Buying Food: Check expiration dates to see how long the food will be safe to store and safe to eat. When buying produce or deli foods, make sure they are fresh and have been properly refrigerated in the store. At home, promptly store the foods at their proper temperature.

When Preparing Food: Thaw meat and frozen food safely either in the refrigerator overnight or in the microwave. (Thawing food at room temperature causes it to defrost unevenly and is not recommended.) Keep uncooked (raw) foods away from cooked ones. Use separate or clean work surfaces, cutting boards, and utensils for raw and cooked food. Remove any pesticide residue from fresh fruit and vegetables by rinsing them in tap water before you eat or cut them.

Cooking Food: When cooking, make sure the food is fully cooked throughout before serving and eating it. Avoid rare foods. Red meats, poultry, and pork should not be pink in color when they are cut open.

Storing Food: Keep hot foods hot and cold foods cold. Do not leave cooked food out at room temperature for more than one hour. When picnicking, be sure to keep cold food in a cooler at cool temperatures, and keep all food away from the sunlight.

Handling Leftovers: Keep leftovers sealed tightly with plastic wrap or in airtight containers. Promptly store them in the freezer or refrigerator.

How Do Foods Become Unsafe?: Every surface contains microscopic substances called bacteria. These bacteria can be found on a person's hands, kitchen counters, utensils, sponges, and even in foods themselves. Some bacteria won't hurt people, and some are actually good, but others can cause food poisoning that can make people sick. By following safe food handling procedures, you can help keep your foods safe to eat.

probably heard of, like protein, fat, carbohydrates, vitamins, minerals, and even water. All these nutrients work together in our bodies to help us grow, have energy, and stay healthy.

Food Pyramid

In order to help us understand the importance of eating foods for good nutrition without having to study all the nutrients, the United States Department of Agriculture, or USDA, has developed a food pyramid that shows how much of each type of food people should eat each day. You might already know about the food pyramid from school, or from reading food product labels.

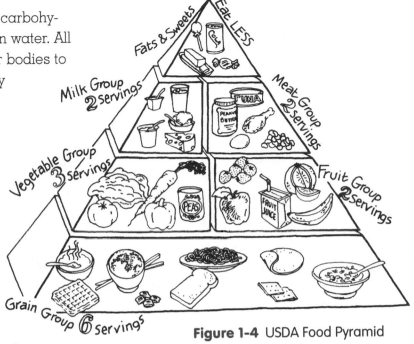

Figure 1-4 USDA Food Pyramid

Breads and Cereals

When you look at the food pyramid, you might notice that the biggest part of it is at the bottom, in the bread and cereal group. We need to eat most of our food from this group, at least six servings each day. Some good foods to choose from this group are whole grains, like whole wheat breads, cereals, brown rice, and pasta. Bread and cereal foods give us lots of energy.

Fruits and Vegetables

As you move up the food pyramid, the next groups are known as the fruit and vegetable groups. At least five servings of fruits and vegetables should be eaten every day. It doesn't matter if one day you eat three fruits and two vegetables, then on another day eat one fruit and four vegetables. What's important is eating many different foods from these groups. Fruits and vegetables give you lots of vitamins, minerals, and antioxidants, and help your body stay healthy in many different ways.

Read a Nutrition Label

Look on food products for the part of the label marked "Nutrition Facts." The nutrition section provides people with information on how much nutrition is found in any particular food. Here, you will find information about how many servings are in the package, how big a serving is, how many calories there are in a serving, and how much nutrition this food provides.

Looking at Figure 1-5, can you find the number of servings, the calories each serving has, and how much sugar this food contains? The nutrients listed here are measured in grams and milligrams, which are very small amounts but very important to your body. Some vitamins and minerals are also listed by percentages. These percentages tell people how much of these vitamins and minerals this food contributes based on a total day's requirement.

Can you figure out how much of your day's requirement of vitamin A and calcium this food gives you?

Now find a food product at home and see if you can understand the Nutrition Facts of that food, too.

Nutrition Facts

Serving Size 1 cup (228g)
Servings Per Container 2

Amount Per Serving

Calories 250   Calories from Fat 110

	% Daily Value*
Total Fat 12g	18%
Saturated Fat 3g	15%
Cholesterol 30mg	10%
Sodium 470mg	20%
Total Carbohydrate 31g	10%
Dietary Fiber 0g	0%
Sugars 5g	
Protein 5g	
Vitamin A	4%
Vitamin C	2%
Calcium	20%
Iron	4%

* Percent Daily Values are based on a 2,000 calorie diet. Your Daily Values may be higher or lower depending on your calorie needs:

		Calories	2,000	2,500
Total Fat	Less than		65g	80g
Sat Fat	Less than		20g	25g
Cholesterol	Less than		300mg	300mg
Sodium	Less than		2,400mg	2,400mg
Total Carbohydrate			300g	375g
Dietary Fiber			25g	30g

Figure 1-5 Nutrition Facts label

Proteins

Next, you will see the meat or protein-rich group. Beef, pork, chicken, fish, eggs, beans, and nuts are all rich in protein. Foods in this group help build our muscles and keep us strong. People don't need too many foods from this group . . . only about two servings each day.

Dairy

The dairy group is next to the meat group. Dairy foods include products like milk, cheese, and yogurt. These foods give us protein, like meat does, but they help our bones grow and stay strong, too. They also give us healthy teeth. Two to three servings a day are recommended from the dairy group.

Sweets

Finally, move to the very top of the food pyramid where you will find a tiny group called the fats, oils, and sweets group. This group contains sugar and fat-rich foods like candy, cookies, pastries, and soft drinks. People don't need many foods from here at all. In fact, there is not even a daily requirement! Just limit the amount of foods you eat that have a lot of sugar or fat in them, because they have very few nutrients. They do taste good, but don't help bodies grow or stay healthy. Try to choose foods from the other groups first, before choosing foods from this group.

Now you know a little bit about nutrition. Do you think you could keep track of how well you eat from the food pyramid for one day? Here is a sample worksheet for you to use.

My Food Pyramid

For Breakfast I Ate:
....
....
....

For Lunch I Ate:
....
....
....

For Dinner I Ate:
....
....
....

For Snacks I Ate:
....
....
....

Food Group:
....
....
....

Food Group:
....
....
....

Food Group:
....
....
....

Food Group:
....
....
....

Now Add Up Your Total:

Breads/Cereal Group: ....

Fruit/Vegetable Group: ....

Protein Group: ....

Dairy Group: ....

Fats/Sugar Group: ....

How well did you do? Are you eating what you should each day and getting a wide variety of nutrients? If you are, congratulations—you are a good eater! If you are not, see if you can change some of your eating habits and work toward a healthier diet. Good luck and healthy eating!

Nutrition Buzz Words . . . What Do They Mean?

Nutrition is the study of the foods people eat and the substances that are found in them. People often talk about many things found in foods, sometimes you might know what these words mean and other times you might not. To help you learn about the common words talked about today, here is a list of the hot "buzz" words and what they mean.

Calcium—a nutrient, found most often in dairy foods, that helps keep bones and teeth strong

Calorie—the measurement of energy found in food

Carbohydrate—a nutrient that consists of sugars and starches and provides your body's main energy source

Cholesterol—a white, waxy type of fat made by the body and found in foods that come from animals.

Fat—a nutrient that is stored in the body, helps provide energy, and supplies important vitamins. It also makes food taste good by giving it a smooth or crispy texture. Fat is found in meat, milk, nuts, fried foods, and sweets. People need fat—just not too much!

Fiber—a substance that cannot be digested by the body. Fiber helps to excrete (or remove) wastes from our bodies by pushing food through the intestine.

Iron—a nutrient the body needs to keep blood strong

Nutrients—various substances, like vitamins and minerals, found in food. Our body needs over fifty different nutrients each day.

Nutrition—the study of the food we eat and how our bodies use it

Protein—a nutrient that supplies energy, and builds muscles, skin, and body organs

As you learn more about nutrition, you will learn many more words. This is just a sample of the types of things you should know. As you grow up, you will understand much more about how the foods you eat make a difference in your overall health. That's why people often say, "You are what you eat."

Setting a Table

Whether you want to cook for your friends or help out your family, you will want to know the correct way to set a table. Some table settings will have more utensils on them than others. It all depends on how fancy or formal your dinner is going to be. Here are drawings of formal and casual table settings.

Figure 1-6 Casual Table Setting: This simple setting works well for a quiet family dinner or lunch.

Figure 1-7 Formal Table Setting (appetizer, soup, main course, dessert): Formal settings can be different depending on how many courses you serve, and how many plates or utensils you have to use. Formal settings are best for very special occasions, like celebrations and holidays.

Step-by-Step Directions for Setting a Table

1. Begin with a placemat (if you choose).
2. Place the plate in the center of the placemat.
3. Set the knife and spoon to the right of the plate with the blade of the knife facing toward the inside. The knife should be set closest to the plate.
4. Fold a napkin and set it on the plate.
5. Place the fork just to the right (or on top) of the napkin.
6. Set the drinking glass on the right, above the knife.
7. If you are using a bowl, it can be placed on top of the dinner plate or to the left of the setting, just above the fork.

Formal place setting may require more utensils, and more dishes (like salad forks or bread plates). The thing for you to remember is that as you go through the meal, you will be using your utensils "from the outside in" so the salad fork goes outside (to the left) of the dinner fork, and the soup spoon goes outside (to the right) of the table knife. Refer to the drawing (Figure 1-7) for more help in setting the table for a formal meal.

Food Expressions

People often use food expressions in everyday conversations. Here are some common ones you will likely hear. Can you think of more?

Are you chicken?
As easy as pie
Beef it up
Big apple
Big cheese
Bowl a turkey
Brain the size of a pea
Bring home the bacon
Couch potato
Don't clam up
Eat your words
Fishing for information
Fruit of the earth
He's hen-pecked
Make mincemeat out of me
Milk it for all it's worth
No baloney
Pig headed
Relish the moment
Selling like hotcakes
Spill the beans
Squash them
That's corny
Top banana
Turn to jelly
You shrimp
Your goose is cooked

A Tasty Puzzle!

OK, you can't actually eat this puzzle, but you can use your "noodle" to cook up some answers. P.S. We left you a T-A-S-T-Y hint!

ACROSS
2. This form of fat might be listed on a food label as "vegetable _____."
4. These are the parts of food that your body uses to grow, have energy, and stay healthy. Junk foods have very few of them.
8. To find out what the ingredients are in your food, read the _____!

DOWN
1. You need six to eight glasses of this nutrient every day.
3. Bees make this form of sugar.
5. It's OK to have "junk food" once in a while as a special _____.
6. Squirrels like this food, which contains a lot of protein and fat.
7. Foods at the tip of the food pyramid are loaded with fat and _____.

Ahh, my favorite nutrient!

A hot potato!

What do you call a stolen yam?

Chapter 2
Wake Up to a Good Breakfast

Breakfast is called the most important meal of the day. That's because it gives you your first energy for the day. It gives you energy to work, play, think, read, and concentrate.

The word breakfast comes from the term "breaking the fast," meaning the foods you eat break the fast from all the hours of not eating since the night before. Even though many foods are considered breakfast foods, you can eat almost anything to break that fast.

Breakfast Scrambles

First, unscramble all the words in the frying pan. Then use them to complete the riddles.
HINT: These breakfast orders are silly, not normal! Think twice before you write your answers down.

Use the space below to work out the breakfast words from the frying pan:

SHOGT   SGEG
ASTOT   OACEBN
NBCOA   EGLS

What does a dog have for breakfast?

Woofles!

1. What does a centipede have for breakfast?
   _ _ _ _ _ _ AND _ _ _ _ _

2. What does a lighthouse keeper have for breakfast?
   _ _ _ _ _ _ _ AND _ _ _ _ _

3. What does a spook have for breakfast?
   _ _ _ _ _ _   _ _ _ _ _

Breakfast Crepes

French crepes taste delicious with fresh fruit. Strawberries, peaches, raspberries, or blueberries make this breakfast a special treat.

▶ Difficulty: Medium

Makes 6 large crepes

3 eggs
1½ cups milk
2 Tbsp. butter or margarine, melted
1 Tbsp. sugar
½ tsp. salt

1 cup flour
2 tsp. oil
1 Tbsp. confectioners' (powdered) sugar, optional
Syrup, optional

Did You Know...

Food Trivia

Bon appetit is French for "enjoy your meal."

Flip It!

Flipping crepes may take some practice. You may need some help at first, or you may need to use two spatulas. Be careful!

Tip

1. In a large bowl, beat the eggs with a whisk.
2. Add the milk, melted butter, sugar, and salt. Mix well.
3. Add in the flour. Mix until smooth.
4. In a large skillet, heat a small amount of the oil (about 1 teaspoon) over medium heat.
5. Pour about ½ cup of the batter into the hot skillet. While holding the handle of the skillet, tilt it to spread the batter around the entire bottom of the pan.
6. Cook the crepe until the bottom begins to brown and bubbles form on the top. Use a spatula to flip the crepe over and cook the other side until it is brown too.
7. Carefully, slide the crepe out of the skillet and stack it on a plate. Continue cooking the remaining crepes until all the batter is used up. Use additional oil in the pan, as needed.

When all the crepes are finished, roll each crepe up to serve. Add fruit or sprinkle with confectioners' sugar or syrup, if you'd like.

Why bread rises?

Many breads contain yeast, a fungus that allows bread to expand or rise. Yeast feeds off of sugar (included in most bread recipes), and in doing so gives off carbon dioxide gas. As the gas is released, it gets trapped inside the bread dough before it is cooked, and causes the dough to expand, or "rise." You can watch this happen during the rising process of yeast breads.

How do you drop an egg for ten feet without breaking it?

Drop it for eleven feet— it won't break for the first ten!

Poppin' Popovers

Popovers are so easy to make, and are more fun than regular muffins. You can make them in a special popover pan, a muffin tin pan, or even small custard cups.

▶ Difficulty: Medium

Makes 6 popovers

3 eggs
1 cup milk
3 Tbsp. butter, melted
1 cup flour
Dash of salt

1. Preheat the oven to 375 degrees. Spray the muffin tin pan (popover pan or individual custard cups) with cooking spray.
2. In a large bowl, beat the eggs with a whisk.
3. Add the milk, melted butter, flour, and salt, and stir until the mixture is smooth.
4. Pour the egg mixture into the prepared pan so each cup is about 2/3 full.
5. Bake 25–35 minutes, or until your popovers are puffed up and golden brown.

Remove popovers from pan. Serve warm or cold, with butter or jam.

Cinnamon Raisin French Toast

If you can't find cinnamon raisin bread, use regular raisin bread. Make your own cinnamon flavor by adding 1 tablespoon of sugar and ½ teaspoon of cinnamon to your egg mixture.

▶ Difficulty: Medium

Makes 8 slices of French toast or 4 servings

2 eggs
⅓ cup milk
2 Tbsp. butter
8 slices cinnamon raisin bread
Syrup, optional
Confectioners' (powdered) sugar, optional

1. In pie plate or large bowl, beat the eggs and milk with a whisk.

2. In large skillet, melt 1 Tbsp. of the butter over medium heat.

3. Dip the slices of bread in the egg mixture, coating both sides.

4. Put 2–4 slices of bread into the heated skillet at a time, and cook 1–2 minutes on each side until golden brown. Continue with additional butter and slices of bread.

Serve with your favorite syrup or sprinkled with confectioners' sugar.

Crack an Egg

Gently crack the eggshell on the edge of a cup or bowl; let the shell crack into two parts and, holding onto the shell, let the egg drop easily into the bowl. It's always best to crack an egg on the edge of a clear glass cup (like a glass measuring cup) or small glass bowl, and drop the yolk and white into the cup or bowl before putting it together with other ingredients. That way, if the cracked egg has any eggshell in it, or if it is a bad egg that has blood or a red spot in it, you can throw it away before it ruins your other ingredients.

Know the Basics

Bagel #1

Figure out the topping on this bagel by reading the letters in a circle. The trick is to know which letter comes first, and whether to read to the right, or to the left!

The **A**B**C**s of Kitchen Safety and Fun . . .

Ask an adult before cooking

Apple Cinnamon Oatmeal

You can also add raisins to this oatmeal, if you would like.

▶ Difficulty: Hard

Makes 4 servings

1 cup rolled oats (not instant)
1 cup milk
1 cup water
1 Tbsp. brown sugar
1 apple, peeled and finely chopped
1 tsp. cinnamon

1. In a large saucepan, combine the oats, milk, water, brown sugar, and chopped apple.
2. Heat the mixture over medium to high heat until it begins to boil, stirring occasionally.
3. Reduce the heat to low and let the mixture simmer for about 2–3 minutes, while continuing to stir.

When the oatmeal thickens and gets a mushy texture to it, remove it from the heat. Pour the oatmeal into bowls and sprinkle with cinnamon before serving.

Homemade Granola

Eat granola as a snack or try it with milk for a quick, healthy breakfast cereal.

▶ Difficulty: Medium

WORDS to KNOW

molasses: the thick, brown syrup that is separated from raw sugar during the refining process

Makes 3 cups of granola

1½ cups rolled oats (not instant)
½ cup shelled sunflower seeds
½ cup raisins or dried cranberries
¼ cup chopped walnuts
¼ cup slivered almonds
2 Tbsp. melted butter
1 Tbsp. oil
1 Tbsp. **molasses**
2 Tbsp. light corn syrup

While cooking, children must be supervised by a responsible adult at all times.

1. Preheat the oven to 375 degrees.
2. In a large bowl, combine the oats, sunflower seeds, raisins, and nuts.
3. In a small bowl, combine the melted butter, oil, molasses, and corn syrup.
4. Pour the butter mixture over the oat mixture and stir it up well.
5. Spread the granola into a 9" × 13" baking pan. Bake 10 minutes.
6. While the granola is cooking, stir the mixture 1–2 times to help it dry out and keep it from burning.

Remove the granola from the oven and stir it again. Let it cool before eating. Store granola in an airtight container.

Cinnamon Breakfast Cake

What a great idea for breakfast or brunch, or even as a snack!

▶ Difficulty: Medium

Makes 12 servings

Batter
2 cups flour
½ cup sugar
1 tsp. baking powder
½ tsp. baking soda
½ tsp. salt
1 Tbsp. melted butter
1 egg, beaten
1½ cups milk

Crumb Topping
¼ cup brown sugar
1 tsp. melted butter
1 tsp. cinnamon
½ cup chopped nuts

1. Preheat the oven to 375 degrees. Spray an 8"-square baking pan with cooking spray.
2. In a large bowl, combine the flour, sugar, baking powder, baking soda, and salt.
3. Add the melted butter, beaten egg, and milk. Mix until just combined. (Do not overstir.)
4. Pour the batter into the prepared baking pan.
5. In a small bowl, mix together the topping ingredients.
6. Sprinkle over the top of the cake batter.
7. Bake 25–30 minutes, or until done.

Bagel #2

Figure out the topping on this bagel by reading the letters in a circle. The trick is to know which letter comes first, and whether to read to the right, or to the left!

Favorite Fried Eggs

Everyone loves fried eggs. Do you know how to make them yourself?

▶ Difficulty: Medium

Makes 2 eggs or 1 serving

2 eggs
1 Tbsp. butter
Salt and pepper, as desired

1. Crack eggs into a small bowl. Try to do this gently so you don't break the yolks. (If the yolks do break, go to page 26 for Cheesy Scrambled Eggs.)
2. In a skillet over medium heat, melt the butter.
3. Pour eggs into the skillet and cook them until the whites set.
4. If you like your eggs "sunny-side up," do not flip the eggs over. Cook them until the eggs are set and not runny. If you like your eggs "over-easy," flip them over and cook until the other side sets.

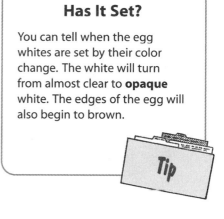

Has It Set?

You can tell when the egg whites are set by their color change. The white will turn from almost clear to **opaque** white. The edges of the egg will also begin to brown.

Tip

WORDS to KNOW

opaque: cloudy; not clear or transparent

Mystery Meal #1 _____

8 slices bread   1/2 cup milk
2 eggs   1 Tbsp. sugar
butter   1/4 tsp. cinnamon

maple syrup

Can you tell what this recipe will make by reading the list of ingredients? Write the name of the finished food at the top of the card.

Cheesy Scrambled Eggs

Try combining several cheeses to create your own favorite cheesy eggs.

▶ Difficulty: Medium

Makes 4 eggs or 2 servings

4 eggs
¼ cup milk
½ tsp. salt
Pinch of pepper
¼ cup shredded cheese, any type
1 Tbsp. butter

1. Crack the eggs into a small bowl.
2. Use a whisk to beat the eggs until they are light yellow and mixed well.
3. Add the milk, salt, pepper, and cheese to the eggs.
4. In a skillet over medium heat, melt the butter.
5. Pour egg mixture into the heated skillet and let it cook. As the eggs start to set, use a spatula to break them up and turn them over.

When eggs are cooked throughout and no longer runny, remove them from the skillet and serve.

Bagel #3

Figure out the topping on this bagel by reading the letters in a circle. The trick is to know which letter comes first, and whether to read to the right, or to the left!

The **ABCs** of Kitchen Safety and Fun . . .

Be sure to read through your reci|

Hard Boiled Eggs

Hard boiled eggs are so easy to make, but many people are afraid to try to make them. Once they are cooked, they can be eaten plain, made into egg salad, or cut up on a chef's salad.

▶ Difficulty: Medium

Makes 2 servings

2 eggs

1. Place the eggs in a small saucepan, and fill the pan with enough water to cover the eggs.
2. Put the saucepan over medium to high heat and bring the water to a boil.
3. Once the water boils, reduce the temperature to low and let the water simmer for 12–15 minutes.
4. Remove the saucepan from the heat and pour cool water into the pan to cool down the eggs. Keep the eggs in the cool water until they are no longer too hot to handle.
5. Gently crack the eggshells and peel them off.

You can serve the eggs whole, sliced on bread, or cut in half.

Did You Know...

Food Trivia

Egg-ceptional facts:

- Eggs from many animals are edible, including eggs from ducks, geese, pigeons, turtles, ostriches, and even crocodiles.
- Caviar is an expensive, luxury food that comes from snail's eggs and tiny black eggs of the sturgeon fish.
- In 1493, Christopher Columbus took chickens on his second voyage to the New World so the sailors would have eggs to eat during their travels.
- To tell whether an egg is raw or has been cooked (without breaking it open), spin it on its pointed end. If it spins, it is cooked; if it falls over, it is raw.
- Since early times, people have decorated eggs to give as gifts at Easter and other times of the year.
- The world's most famous eggs were decorated by Russian jeweler Carl Fabergé.

Fresh Blueberry Muffins

Great for breakfast or just as a snack, these muffins are just as much fun to eat as they are to make.

▶ Difficulty: Medium

Makes 1 dozen muffins

1½ cups fresh blueberries

⅔ cup sugar

1½ cups flour

½ tsp. baking soda

½ tsp. salt

⅓ cup oil

2 eggs, beaten

½ cup milk

1. Preheat oven to 375 degrees. Spray the muffin tin with cooking spray.
2. Put the blueberries into a colander and rinse them off.
3. In a large bowl, combine the sugar, flour, baking soda, and salt.
4. In a small bowl, combine the oil, beaten eggs, and milk.
5. Add the liquid ingredients into the dry ingredients and stir together until they are just blended. (Do not overmix.)
6. Fold the blueberries into the batter.
7. Pour the batter into the prepared pan, so each cup is about ⅔ full.
8. Bake 18–20 minutes, or until muffins are lightly browned and cooked throughout.

You can serve the muffins fresh from the oven! After they have cooled, cover them with waxed paper to keep them fresh.

Test to Be Sure

To test for doneness, insert a toothpick into the center of the muffins. If the toothpick comes out clean, the muffins are done. If there is batter on the toothpick, the muffins need to cook another 1–2 minutes. Then, test again with a clean toothpick.

Know the Basics

What does a beaver in a hurry eat for breakfast?

Instant oakmeal!

Puffy Buttermilk Pancakes

Watch these pancakes puff up as they cook. Make them as a weekend treat, but be sure to save the extras to reheat for breakfast during the week.

▶ Difficulty: Medium

Makes 1½ dozen pancakes

2 cups flour
2 Tbsp. sugar
1 tsp. baking powder
½ tsp. baking soda
1½ cups reduced fat
    buttermilk

1 egg, lightly beaten
2 Tbsp. oil
syrup

1. In a large bowl, combine the flour, sugar, baking powder, and baking soda.
2. Add the buttermilk and the beaten egg. Mix together with a whisk until smooth.
3. In a large skillet, heat half of the oil. Drop pancake batter, about the size of 2 tablespoonfuls, onto the hot skillet.
4. Cook until the edges become brown and the batter becomes bubbly.
5. Flip pancakes over and cook until the other side is browned, too. Continue cooking the rest of the pancakes until all the batter is used up. (Add more oil to the pan as you need to.)

Serve pancakes with your favorite syrup or fresh fruit.

Bagel #4

Figure out the topping on this bagel by reading the letters in a circle. The trick is to know which letter comes first, and whether to read to the right, or to the left!

Chocolaty Chip Pancakes

Try these as a special treat after a sleepover. They are easy to make, and so much fun to eat!

▶ Difficulty: Medium

Makes 16 pancakes

1 cup flour	1 egg, lightly beaten
1 Tbsp. sugar	2 Tbsp. oil
1 tsp. baking powder	Syrup
½ cup chocolate chips	**Confectioners'** (powdered)
1 cup milk	**sugar,** optional

1. In a large bowl, combine the flour, sugar, baking powder, and chocolate chips.
2. In a small bowl, combine the milk and the beaten egg.
3. Pour the milk mixture into the flour mixture and mix together with a whisk until smooth.
4. In a large skillet, heat half of the oil. Drop pancake batter, about the size of 2 tablespoonfuls, onto the hot skillet.
5. Cook until the edges become brown and the batter becomes bubbly.
6. Flip pancakes over and cook until the other side is browned, too. Continue cooking the rest of the pancakes until all the batter is used up. (Add more oil to the pan as you need to.)

Serve pancakes with your favorite syrup or sprinkled with confectioners' sugar.

Cheese Danish Roll-Ups

Cheese Danish looks fancy at a bakery, but you can make it easily at home, too.

▶ Difficulty: Hard

Makes 8 cheese danish roll-ups

1 (8-roll) package refrigerated
   crescent rolls
½ cup (4 ounces) softened
   cream cheese
⅓ cup sugar

1 tsp. vanilla
1 Tbsp. butter or margarine,
   melted
2 Tbsp. sugar
½ tsp. cinnamon

Figure out the topping on this bagel by reading the letters in a circle. The trick is to know which letter comes first, and whether to read to the right, or to the left!

1. Preheat the oven to 350 degrees.
2. Unroll the can of crescent rolls and flatten each roll onto a cookie or baking sheet.
3. In a small bowl, use a whisk (or large fork) to mix together the softened cream cheese, ⅓ cup of sugar, and vanilla until smooth.
4. Place a spoonful of the cream cheese mixture on the top of each roll.
5. Roll up the dough to cover the filling.
6. Brush the rolls with the melted butter or margarine, using a pastry brush.
7. In another small bowl, combine the 2 Tbsp. of sugar with the cinnamon. Sprinkle the cinnamon-sugar mixture over the tops of each roll.
8. Bake 8–10 minutes, or until the danish rolls are lightly browned.

Let the danish cool before serving at breakfast. Cover leftovers with waxed paper.

What's Cookin' at Your House?

Are you a creative cook? You may decide to experiment with some of these recipes. If you try something new and everyone likes it, make notes here so you remember what you changed. You can also use this space to write down special recipes from your friends or family.

Recipe Title: ....

Makes .... **servings**

Ingredients:

....

....

....

....

....

Directions:

....

....

....

....

....

....

....

....

....

....

....

What's Cookin' at Your House?

Are you a creative cook? You may decide to experiment with some of these recipes. If you try something new and everyone likes it, make notes here so you remember what you changed. You can also use this space to write down special recipes from your friends or family.

Recipe Title: ....

Makes .... **servings**

Ingredients:

....

....

....

....

....

Directions:

....

....

....

....

....

....

....

....

....

....

....

Chapter 3
Lunches, Sandwiches, and Brown Bag Ideas

L unch time is fun time. It is your time to be creative and have fun with the foods you eat. Whether you are cooking a weekend lunch at home, or packing a lunch for school, find foods that you like best. Try new things and experiment with old favorites. The more you are involved in picking and making your lunch, the better you might like it!

What's for Lunch?

The letters in each column go in the squares directly below them, but not in the same order! Black squares show the spaces between words. When you have correctly filled in the grid, you will have the answer to this riddle:

What's the difference between a person who's not smart and a pizza?

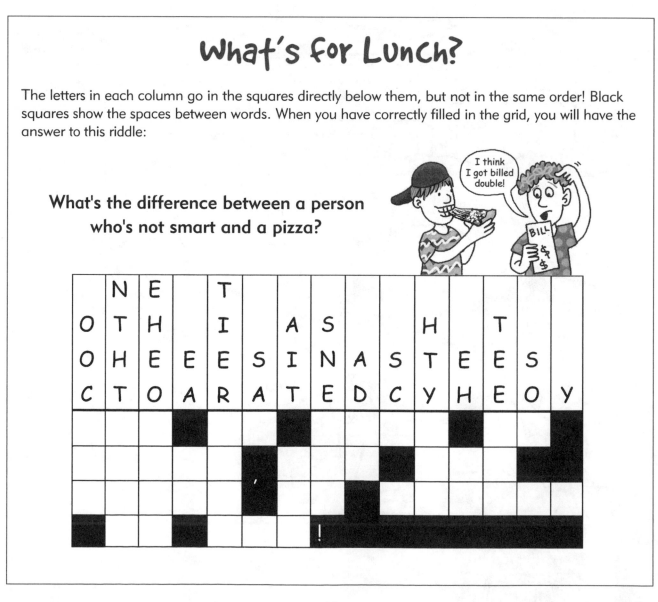

Grilled Cheese and Tomato Sandwich

What's better than a warm and crispy grilled cheese sandwich? Here's a different spin on the old favorite that makes it more nutritious, too.

▶ Difficulty: Medium

Makes 1 sandwich

2 slices bread, white or whole wheat
1 slice American or cheddar cheese
1–2 thin slices of tomato
1 tsp. butter

1. Make a sandwich with the cheese and tomato between the two slices of bread.
2. In a small skillet over medium heat, melt the butter.
3. Place the sandwich in the skillet and cook it for about 2 minutes on each side until the cheese is melted and the bread becomes lightly browned and crispy.

If you are making sandwiches to share, you can serve tomato or vegetable soup, too.

The **ABCs** of
Kitchen Safety and Fun . . .
Clean up the
kitchen as you go.

Make-a-Face Sandwich

When you need a reason to play with food, try this special lunchtime treat. You can also use tuna or egg salad as the sandwich base. The possibilities are endless!

▶ Difficulty: Medium

Makes 4 halves

2 English muffins
½ cup peanut butter
Apple slivers
Strawberry halves
Banana slices

¼ cup raisins or choco- late chips
¼ cup shredded cheddar cheese

1. Place muffin halves on a plate.
2. Wash fruit, and cut it into pieces small enough to fit on an English muffin.
3. Spread peanut butter over each muffin.
4. Decorate your sandwich with any design you can think of, or try this:
   • Place apple slivers to form mouth
   • Place strawberry half above apples to form nose
   • Add banana slices above the strawberry to make the eyes
   • Use raisins or chocolate chips to make eyebrows or mustache
   • Sprinkle cheese on top to make hair

These are especially fun to make with (or for) your friends!

City kid: Do you like raisin bread?

Farmer: Don't know. I've never raised any!

Cheesiest Macaroni and Cheese

A popular favorite from the box—now try it from scratch! It makes a comforting warm meal, or a great cold lunch.

▶ Difficulty: Hard

Play It Safe

Always use potholders or oven mitts to touch hot pans and dishes. You may not realize how hot something is until you've picked it up, so it's always better to start out with your hands protected.

Makes 4 servings

1 cup uncooked elbow
   macaroni
2 Tbsp. butter or margarine
2 Tbsp. flour
¼ tsp. salt
¼ tsp. pepper
¼ tsp. dry mustard

¼ tsp. Worcestershire sauce
1 cup milk
1½ cups sharp cheddar
   cheese, cubed or
   shredded
2 Tbsp. seasoned
   breadcrumbs

1. Preheat the oven to 275 degrees.
2. Cook macaroni noodles in large pot of water according to package directions. Drain in a colander.
3. In a large saucepan over medium heat, melt the butter. Reduce the heat to low.
4. Add the flour, salt, pepper, mustard, and Worcestershire sauce. Stir until smooth.
5. Add the milk and cheese. Continue stirring until the cheese melts and the sauce is creamy and smooth.
6. Stir the macaroni noodles into the cheese sauce.
7. Pour the mixture into a 2-quart casserole dish. Top with the breadcrumbs.
8. Bake 30–40 minutes, or until the casserole is heated through and lightly browned.

Let the casserole dish sit about 5–10 minutes before serving so the cheesy, creamy sauce has a chance to thicken.

Food Trivia

The sandwich was named for the fourth Earl of Sandwich of Britain. He created the sandwich so he could have a meal while playing a card game.

Play It Safe

When Buying Food: Check expiration dates to see how long the food will be safe to store and safe to eat. When buying produce or deli foods, make sure they are fresh and have been properly refrigerated in the store. At home, promptly store the foods at their proper temperature.

Club It Your Way Sandwich

Set up a buffet of options for you and your guests to make sandwiches the way you like them.

▶ Difficulty: Easy

Makes 4 sandwiches

8 slices bread, any type
¼ cup mayonnaise
4 lettuce leaves
½ pound deli-sliced turkey
½ pound deli-sliced ham
1 tomato, thinly sliced
4 slices cheese, any flavor
8 slices bacon, cooked

1. Set out the bread on a plate or in a basket.
2. Using separate small bowls or plates, set out the mayonnaise, lettuce leaves, turkey, ham, tomato slices, cheese, and bacon.
3. Create a sandwich to your own liking.

Serve corn or potato chips and pickles, or look through Chapter 4 (Snack Time) for other ideas of what to serve on the side.

Mini-Pizza in a Flash

Making a mini pizza is about the quickest lunch you can
make. It requires so few ingredients and there are so many
variations to it.

▶ Difficulty: Medium

Makes 2 mini-pizzas

1 English muffin or bagel, split in half
2 Tbsp. pizza, spaghetti, or tomato sauce
¼ cup shredded mozzarella cheese
Meat or vegetable toppings, optional

The **ABC**s of
Kitchen Safety and Fun . . .

Eat foods that are
good for you.

1. Preheat the oven (or toaster oven) to 350 degrees.
2. Place the English muffin or bagel halves on a
cookie sheet or piece of aluminum foil.
3. Spread the pizza sauce over each
English muffin or bagel half. Top
with mozzarella cheese and other
toppings.
4. Bake 5–8 minutes, or until the
cheese is melted.

Like the Make-a-Face Sandwich, you
can make more of this recipe to share
with friends.

While cooking, children must be supervised by a responsible adult at all times.

The **ABCs** of
Kitchen Safety and Fun . . .

Find recipes you
enjoy making.

Tasty Tuna Melt

Tuna melts make a great lunch, or share them as an after-noon snack.

▶ Difficulty: Medium

Makes 4 tuna melt sandwich halves

2 English muffins or bagels, split in half
1 6-ounce can chunk tuna, canned in water, drained
2 Tbsp. mayonnaise
¼ cup shredded or sliced cheese: cheddar, mozzarella, or
    American

1. Preheat the oven, or toaster oven, to 350 degrees.
2. Place English muffin or bagel halves onto a cookie sheet or a sheet of aluminum foil.
3. Use the can opener to open the tuna, then carefully drain the water out.
4. In a small bowl, combine the drained tuna with the mayon-naise. Mix well.
5. Top each English muffin or bagel half with tuna, then with the shredded or sliced cheese.
6. Bake 5–8 minutes, or until the cheese is melted.

What is a sheep's
favorite snack?

A baaaah-loney
sandwich!

Eggy Salad

Egg salad can be used as a sandwich spread or as a dip with crackers. Either way, it tastes so good you'll be surprised how easy it is to make.

▶ Difficulty: Easy

Makes enough for 2 sandwiches or ½ cup dip

2 hard boiled eggs (page 27)
1 Tbsp. mayonnaise
½ tsp. celery salt
¼ tsp. pepper
Paprika, optional

Healthy Habits

Be sure to wash your hands with soap and water before touching food. It is also important to wash your hands after handling raw meat or fish, before you start touching other things.

1. Peel the shells from the hard-boiled eggs and rinse the eggs.
2. Place the eggs in a medium-sized bowl, and mash with a fork or potato masher.
3. Add the mayonnaise, celery salt, and pepper. Mix well.
4. If you'd like, you can sprinkle paprika over the top of the egg salad.

Spread the egg salad over bread slices for a sandwich or place in a small bowl to be used as a dip with crackers, Bag of Bagel Chips (page 48), or Parmesan Pita Chips (page 49).

Mexican Quesadillas

After trying quesadillas with just cheese, be adventurous and add some refried beans, guacamole (page 52), or black olives.

▶ Difficulty: Easy

Makes 2 servings

2 flour **tortillas**
2 Tbsp. shredded cheese, any type
Sour cream or salsa, optional

1. Place one tortilla on a large plate, and sprinkle with the shredded cheese.
2. Top with the second tortilla.
3. Cook in the microwave for about 20–30 seconds until the cheese is melted.

Cool slightly. Use a knife or pizza cutter to cut the tortilla into 6 wedges. Dip in sour cream or salsa, as desired.

Food Trivia

The first microwave was introduced in the late 1940s and called the Radarange.

tortilla: a round, flat, thin cornmeal or wheat flour bread usually eaten with hot topping or filling

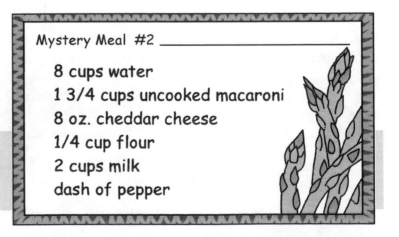

Mystery Meal #2 _____

8 cups water
1 3/4 cups uncooked macaroni
8 oz. cheddar cheese
1/4 cup flour
2 cups milk
dash of pepper

Can you tell what this recipe will make by reading the list of ingredients? Write the name of the finished food at the top of the card.

Snack Time

Most people love to eat snacks, whether they are an after-school treat, or a before-dinner **appetizer.**

Making and sharing snacks is one way you can express your creativity. Snacks should satisfy those "hunger pangs," and carry you on to the next meal. With some imagination, and ingredients you might already have at home, you can have fun today, and snack well tomorrow, too!

Chips and Dip

Oh boy — my favorite!

Color in just the triangles and you will find the answer to this question:

"What's the most popular dip in the United States?"

Peanut Butter Chip Muffins

What a fun snack to make for an after school treat! You can even substitute some chocolate chips for half the peanut butter ones for a different twist.

▶ Difficulty: Medium

WORDS to KNOW

appetizer: a food or drink that stimulates the appetite and is usually served before a meal

Makes 1 dozen muffins

1 cup smooth peanut butter	1½ cups flour
1 egg	1 Tbsp. baking powder
¼ cup sugar	½ cup peanut butter chips
¼ cup brown sugar	Chocolate icing or melted
1 cup milk	chocolate, optional

1. Preheat oven to 375 degrees. Spray a muffin tin pan with cooking spray or line the cups with paper liners.
2. In a bowl, combine the peanut butter, egg, sugar, brown sugar, and milk, using an electric mixer to beat the ingredients until smooth.
3. Add the flour and baking powder. Mix until just blended. (Do not overmix.)
4. Stir in the peanut butter chips.
5. Pour the batter into the prepared muffin tin pan, so each cup is about ²/₃ full.
6. Bake for 15 minutes, or until the muffins are light brown on top. Cool the muffins in the pan before removing them.

If you'd like, you can drizzle chocolate icing or melted chocolate over the tops of the cooled muffins.

Why popcorn pops?

Each popcorn kernel contains a small drop of water stored inside. When the kernel gets heated, the water inside turns to steam. The kernel then begins to expand as pressure starts to develop inside the hard shell. As a result, the kernel splits open and the popcorn explodes, popping the popcorn and releasing the steam. (Popcorn is a special breed of corn. You cannot take a regular corn kernel and make it pop.)

The **ABCs** of Kitchen Safety and Fun . . .

Get all ingredients out before you start to cook.

Nutty Caramel Corn

This snack is a favorite in the fall, especially around Halloween.

▶ Difficulty: Hard

Makes about 6 cups of caramel corn

1 (3½-ounce bag) plain microwave popcorn, popped	1 cup brown sugar
	½ cup (1 stick) butter
1 cup dry-roasted, salted peanuts	½ cup corn syrup
	¼ tsp. salt

1. Preheat the oven to 200 degrees. Spray a 9" × 13" baking pan with cooking spray.
2. In a large bowl, combine the popped popcorn and nuts.
3. In a medium saucepan, combine the brown sugar, butter, corn syrup, and salt.
4. Heat over medium to high heat until mixture is melted and smooth, stirring constantly.
5. Remove from heat after 4–5 minutes.
6. Pour caramel mixture over the popcorn and nuts, mixing well.
7. Spread the popcorn mixture out into the prepared cookie sheet.
8. Bake 1 hour, stirring every 15 minutes.

Let the caramel corn cool before you serve it. If you have any left over, store it in an airtight container or a resealable bag.

Quick Eating S'mores

You don't need a campfire to make this all-time favorite outdoor snack. Here's a quick version that's good anytime.

▶ Difficulty: Easy

Makes 1 s'more

2 graham cracker squares   1 chocolate candy bar square
1 large marshmallow

1. Place the marshmallow and chocolate square between the 2 graham cracker squares and make a "sandwich."
2. Place your "sandwich" on a plate and cover with a paper towel.
3. Cook for 10 seconds in the microwave, until the marshmallow puffs and melts slightly.

Take the first bite carefully, and keep a glass of milk handy. There's nothing like cold milk to wash down chocolaty treats!

Did You Know...

Food Trivia

Milk it for all it's worth.

- The average American drinks twenty-five gallons of milk every year.
- Milk is the first food babies and many animals drink.
- In early times, milk and dairy foods were called "white meat."
- Cows make milk from eating grass and drinking water.
- Milk is a good source of calcium, a mineral that is important for strong bones and teeth.
- Milk has long been a symbol of wealth. The Bible even uses the term "flowing with milk and honey," often when describing rich countries.

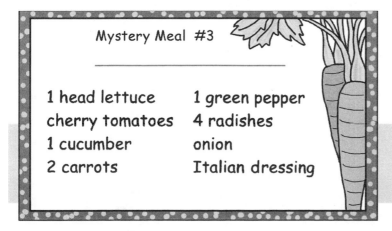

Mystery Meal #3

1 head lettuce   1 green pepper
cherry tomatoes   4 radishes
1 cucumber   onion
2 carrots   Italian dressing

Can you tell what this recipe will make by reading the list of ingredients? Write the name of the finished food at the top of the card.

Bag of Bagel Chips

Bagel chips are such a fun snack to have handy. Here's an easy way to make your own. Try using cinnamon raisin or other fruited flavors for a sweeter chip.

▶ Difficulty: Hard

Makes about 20–24 bagel chips

3–4 leftover bagels, 1–2 days old

1. Preheat the oven to 350 degrees.
2. Slice the bagel in thin circle slices (like chips), about ¼-inch thick each.
3. Lay the bagel slices onto a cookie sheet. Place the cookie sheet in the oven and bake for 10–12 minutes, or until the bagel slices are lightly browned and crispy.

Keep cooled bagel chips in an airtight container and grab them for a quick snack.

The **ABCs** of Kitchen Safety and Fun . . .

Handle appliances carefully!

While cooking, children must be supervised by a responsible adult at all times.

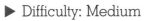
Parmesan Pita Chips

These tasty snacks are quick to make when you have some extra pita bread you need to use.

▶ Difficulty: Medium

Makes about 4 dozen pita chips

4 pieces pita bread
6 Tbsp. oil
½ cup grated Parmesan cheese
1½ Tbsp. sesame seeds

1. Preheat the oven to 425 degrees.
2. Split each pita bread in half, then use a pizza cutter to cut each round into 6 wedges.
3. Place wedges on a cookie sheet.
4. In a small bowl, combine the Parmesan cheese and sesame seeds.
5. Brush the oil on the top of each pita wedge.
6. Sprinkle pita wedges with Parmesan-sesame mixture.
7. Bake 5–10 minutes, or until light brown.

You can serve your pita chips with a dip or **hummus** (a chickpea spread), or store them in an airtight container for snacking any time.

hummus: A Middle Eastern dish that is a mixture of mashed chickpeas, garlic, and other ingredients, used especially as a dip for pita

The Apple Barrel

Marco, Jake, Ben, and Ethan are best friends who share everything. Today they went apple picking and came home with thirteen apples. Some of the apples are really big, and some are pretty tiny. How can the four boys divide the apples evenly if they don't have a scale with which to weigh them?

Take-Along Trail Mix

Trail mix is so versatile you can create your own versions, too. Try adding some yogurt-covered raisins, dry cereal, fish crackers, chocolate-coated candies, or even popcorn.

▶ Difficulty: Easy

Makes 2 cups of trail mix

½ cup small pretzel sticks or twists
½ cup raisins
½ cup peanuts
¼ cup sunflower seeds
¼ cup chocolate chips

In a large bowl, combine all ingredients together.

If you want to serve trail mix at a party, or keep a supply for packing a snack, try doubling the recipe. (Use twice the amount of ingredients.) Store the supply in an airtight container or resealable bag.

Food Trivia

Nuts are actually a dry type of fruit that grow in a hard shell.

The **ABCs** of Kitchen Safety and Fun . . . **I**magine what you can do!

Can you tell what this recipe will make by reading the list of ingredients? Write the name of the finished food at the top of the card.

Mystery Meal #4 _____

1/2 cup butter
1 cup brown sugar
2 eggs

1 1/2 tsp. vanilla
2 1/2 cups flour
1 tsp. baking soda
1/2 tsp. salt
6 oz. semi-sweet chocolate pieces

Never Enough Nachos

This is so easy to make, you'll never run out.

▶ Difficulty: Hard

While cooking, children must be supervised by a responsible adult at all times.

Makes 8–10 servings

1 pound ground beef
1 cup prepared salsa
2 cups tortilla chips
½ cup sour cream
1 medium tomato, chopped

4 green onions, chopped
½ cup shredded lettuce
1 cup shredded cheddar
  cheese

1. Heat the oven to 350 degrees.
2. In a large skillet, cook the ground beef for 8–10 minutes until it is cooked throughout. Drain the ground beef, then place it in a large bowl.
3. Add the salsa, and mix well.
4. Chop the tomatoes and onion (or get an adult to help), and shred lettuce into small pieces. Place in separate small bowls.
5. In a 2-quart casserole, layer the ground beef and the other ingredients starting at the bottom:
  • Tortilla chips
  • Ground beef
  • Sour cream
  • Tomatoes
  • Onions
  • Lettuce
  • Shredded cheese
6. Bake 20–30 minutes, or until the cheese completely melts.

Let the nachos cool slightly (for 5–10 minutes) before putting them out.
Serve with additional tortilla chips.

WORDS to KNOW

pitted: Without the center pit (as in peaches, olives, or avocados)

Smashing Idea

To mash an avocado, use a fork or potato masher and mash it until it is smooth.

Tip

What tastes better before it's cooked?

Burnt toast

Guacamole Dip with Tortillas

Jazz up your nachos with some guacamole, too.

▶ Difficulty: Medium

Makes about 1½ cups of guacamole

1 plum tomato, chopped
2 ripe avocados, peeled, **pitted,** and mashed
1 Tbsp. chopped onion
1 Tbsp. lime juice
1 tsp. chopped garlic
¼ tsp. salt
Dash of pepper
Tortilla chips

1. Chop the tomato (or get someone to help you). Place the chopped tomatoes in a medium bowl.
2. Add mashed avocado and remaining ingredients, and mix well.

For a snack, serve with tortilla chips, or as a condiment for any southwestern style food (including the Mexican Quesadillas on page 42).

Chocolate Chip Granola

Not only is this fun to eat by itself, it makes a great topping for yogurt and ice cream.

▶ Difficulty: Medium

The **ABC**s of Kitchen Safety and Fun . . . **J**ust have fun!

Makes 5 cups of granola

3½ cups rolled oats (not instant)	½ cup chocolate chips
¼ cup oil	½ cup white chocolate chips
¼ cup honey	½ cup sunflower seeds
1 tsp. vanilla	½ cup slivered almonds

1. Preheat the oven to 300 degrees, and spray a 9" × 13" baking pan with cooking spray.
2. In a large bowl, combine all ingredients, and mix well.
3. Spread out granola mixture in the prepared pan.
4. Bake 15–20 minutes, or until lightly browned and heated throughout.

Store cooled granola in an airtight container.

Mystery Meal #5 _____

2 hard boiled eggs
1 Tbsp. mayonnaise
1/2 tsp. celery salt
1/4 tsp. black pepper
paprika (optional)
4 slices whole wheat bread

Can you tell what this recipe will make by reading the list of ingredients? Write the name of the finished food at the top of the card.

Chapter 5
Soothing Soups

You may think that soups are "old food," but you will probably be surprised by how much fun they are once you try a few. A soothing soup can be a meal by itself, or the first course of a larger meal if you want to add a special touch.

On a rainy Saturday, you can fix soup and sandwiches for your family, and freeze the extra. Once you become a soup wizard, you may find a new favorite among these choices.

The Soup Pot

Put a different letter of the alphabet into each of the empty boxes to make the names of familiar soups and soup ingredients. The letter might be at the beginning, middle, or end of the word. Each letter on the list will be used only once. Cross each letter off the list as you use it. HINT: We gave you one important ingredient to get you started.

A D H I M M N N N O O O S X̶ R R

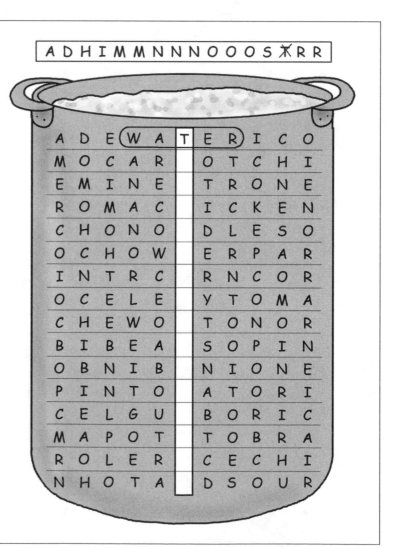

A	D	E	(W	A	T	E	R)	I	C	O
M	O	C	A	R		O	T	C	H	I
E	M	I	N	E		T	R	O	N	E
R	O	M	A	C		I	C	K	E	N
C	H	O	N	O		D	L	E	S	O
O	C	H	O	W		E	R	P	A	R
I	N	T	R	C		R	N	C	O	R
O	C	E	L	E		Y	T	O	M	A
C	H	E	W	O		T	O	N	O	R
B	I	B	E	A		S	O	P	I	N
O	B	N	I	B		N	I	O	N	E
P	I	N	T	O		A	T	O	R	I
C	E	L	G	U		B	O	R	I	C
M	A	P	O	T		T	O	B	R	A
R	O	L	E	R		C	E	C	H	I
N	H	O	T	A		D	S	O	U	R

Creamy Corn Chowder

This hearty soup makes a cozy meal on a cold day.

▶ Difficulty: Hard

Makes 6 servings

1 Tbsp. oil	¼ tsp. pepper
1 onion, finely chopped	2 (15¼ -ounce) cans corn, drained
3 medium potatoes, peeled and chopped	2 cups milk
2 cups water	2 Tbsp. butter or margarine
½ tsp. salt	2 Tbsp. cornstarch

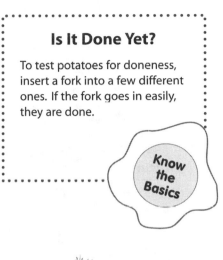

The ABCs of Kitchen Safety and Fun . . .
Keep counters clean.

1. In a large saucepan, heat the oil over medium heat.
2. Add the onion and cook for about 5 minutes, stirring frequently.
3. Add the potatoes, water, salt, and pepper.
4. Turn up the heat until the mixture begins to boil.
5. When the soup starts to boil, reduce it to a simmer and continue to cook for about 20 minutes, or until the potatoes are tender.
6. In a separate bowl mix the cornstarch with a little warm water to avoid clumps.
7. Add the corn, milk, and butter, and stir in the cornstarch to help thicken the soup.
8. Continue simmering for another 20 minutes, stirring occasionally.

Cool slightly before serving. Try your chowder with a salad, Down-Home Cornbread (page 86), and fruit for a complete meal.

Vegetable Tortilla Soup

Make this as mild or as spicy as you wish, depending on what you and your guests or family like.

▶ Difficulty: Hard

Makes 4 servings

1 tsp. oil
1 onion, chopped
1 small tomato, chopped
¼ cup chopped green pepper
¼ cup chopped red pepper
1 tsp. lime juice

4 cups vegetable (or chicken) broth
½ tsp. salt
Dash pepper
Dash hot pepper sauce
1 ripe avocado, chopped
Tortilla chips

1. In a large saucepan or **Dutch oven,** heat the oil over medium heat.
2. Add the onions and cook for about 5 minutes, stirring frequently.
3. Add the tomato and peppers. Cook for about 2 minutes until the vegetables are softened.
4. Add the lime juice, broth, salt, pepper, and hot pepper sauce.
5. Cook until fully heated throughout.

Pour soup into individual bowls, and top with chopped avocados and tortilla chips, as desired.

Did You Know...

Why does cutting onions cause tears?

Onions contain a type of oil or organic molecule called amino acid sulfoxides. When you peel, cut, or crush an onion, enzymes called allinases are released. The enzymes cause the oil to change to sulfenic acids, and the sulfenic acid vapors are what cause the eyes to tear.

WORDS to KNOW

Dutch oven: a heavy pot with a tight-fitting domed cover

Tasty Tomato Soup

Tomato soup has been a family staple for years. It's just as easy to make from scratch as it is from a can.

▶ Difficulty: Hard

Makes 4 servings

10–12 ripe tomatoes, peeled
   and chopped
1 Tbsp. oil
1 onion, chopped
3 garlic cloves, chopped

1 (14½-ounce) can
   vegetable broth
1 (6-ounce) can tomato
   paste
1 tsp. dried basil

> ### Tender Trick
>
> You can tell when an onion is tender because it begins to turn clear in color.
>
> ### Pesky Peels
>
> To peel the skin off of the tomatoes, use a small, sharp knife that can get under the skin easily. Because peeling with a paring knife takes a lot of practice, an adult may have to help you the first couple of times.

Tip

1. Peel and chop the tomatoes, then place them in a large bowl and set them aside.
2. In large saucepan, heat the oil over medium heat.
3. Add the onion and garlic and cook for about 3 minutes, or until the onion is tender.
4. Add the tomatoes, cover the pan, and cook for about 5 minutes to soften the tomatoes.
5. Add the vegetable broth and tomato paste.
6. Bring the mixture to a boil over high heat, then reduce it to a simmer. Cover the pan again for another 10–15 minutes.
7. Pour the soup into a blender or food processor, 1 cup at a time. Do not overfill the blender. If you put too much into the blender at once, the hot liquid will overflow when you turn it on.
8. Blend the mixture until it is smooth.

Pour blended soup into serving bowls to serve and sprinkle with basil. Continue with remaining portions. It may be helpful to prepare this soup in advance, and transfer the blended soup to a new saucepan to keep warm on the stove.

Chicken Soup Like Mom's

Chicken soup is perfect for lunch, or as an addition to any meal. Of course, it's also perfect when you might just feel under the weather.

▶ Difficulty: Hard

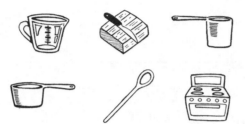

Makes 4 servings

1 quart (4 cups) water
4 chicken-flavored bouillon cubes
2 carrots, sliced
2 celery stalks, chopped
½ cup pasta or rice
1 cup chopped chicken (use leftover chicken meat or 1 skinless, boneless chicken breast, cooked)

1. In a large saucepan, boil the water.
2. Add bouillon cubes, carrots, and celery, stirring until the cubes have dissolved.
3. Reduce the heat to a simmer and add the pasta or rice.
4. Continue cooking for 15–20 minutes, or until the vegetables are tender and the pasta or rice is cooked. Add the chicken and simmer for 1–2 minutes more.

If you make a double recipe, freeze half in airtight plastic containers to reheat at another time.

The **ABCs** of Kitchen Safety and Fun . . . **L**earn your way around the kitchen.

Testing Veggies

To test for doneness, insert a fork into the vegetables. If the fork goes in easily, they are done.

Know the Basics

Chili in No Time

Add some crackers or tortilla chips, and you have meal in itself. This chili can also be made without the macaroni noodles, if you prefer.

▶ Difficulty: Hard

WORDS to KNOW

garnish: To add colorful, but tasty, "decorations" to a meal

Makes 6 servings

8 ounces macaroni noodles
1 pound lean ground beef
1 (15-ounce) can kidney
   beans, drained and rinsed
1 (15-ounce) can beef broth

1 (14½-ounce) can chopped
   tomatoes, do not drain
1 (6-ounce) can tomato paste
1 Tbsp. chili powder
½ tsp. pepper

¼ tsp. cumin
Chopped onions, shredded
   cheese, optional toppings

1. Prepare macaroni noodles according to package directions. Drain.
2. In a large skillet or saucepan, brown the ground beef, and drain the excess fat.
3. Add the remaining ingredients and bring the ground beef mixture to a boil.
4. Reduce the heat to a simmer (or low heat) and continue to cook another 10–15 minutes, until the chili thickens.

You can serve the chili over macaroni noodles, and **garnish** with chopped onions or shredded cheese, if you desire.

While cooking, children must be supervised by a responsible adult at all times.

What's Cookin' at Your House?

Are you a creative cook? You may decide to experiment with some of these recipes. If you try something new and everyone likes it, make notes here so you remember what you changed. You can also use this space to write down special recipes from your friends or family.

Recipe Title: ....

Makes .... **servings**

Ingredients:

....

....

....

....

....

Directions:

....

....

....

....

....

....

....

....

....

....

....

Chapter 6
What's for Dinner?

long time ago, dinnertime was always "family time." A lot of families are trying to spend meals together again because it's the one time during the day when everyone is sitting in the same place!

During family dinners, you can talk about your day, have a good conversation with your parents and siblings, and have a good meal, too. If dinner is a busy time in your house, offer to help and use these great dinner ideas.

Oodles of Noodles

Follow the strands of linguini over and under to see which kid gets which meatball.

Not-So-Messy Sloppy Joes

To make these easier—and not-so-messy—to eat, scoop out a small amount of bread from the bun to make a well. Put the Sloppy Joes in the well and top with the other half of the bun. It works!

▶ Difficulty: Hard

Makes 8 servings

1 pound ground beef
1 onion, chopped
2 cups frozen hash brown potatoes
1 (15½-ounce) can Sloppy Joe sauce
8 hamburger buns

1. In a large skillet, brown the ground beef. Drain the extra fat from the ground beef.
2. Add the onions and potatoes.
3. Pour the Sloppy Joe sauce over the top, stirring to blend the ingredients. Cover the skillet.
4. Reduce the heat to low and simmer for 30 minutes.

Serve on hamburger buns or bulky rolls, with fresh salad on the side.

The **ABC**s of Kitchen Safety and Fun . . . **M**ake shopping lists.

Play It Safe

Handling Leftovers: Keep leftovers in a bowl sealed tightly with plastic wrap or in air-tight containers. Promptly store them in the freezer or refrigerator.

Tasty Tacos

Everyone loves tacos in some form or another. Add some gua-camole (page 52) and sour cream, or even substitute soft shells for a change.

▶ Difficulty: Hard

Makes 8 tacos

1 pound ground beef
1 Tbsp. taco seasoning
2 Tbsp. water
1 tomato, chopped
½ cup shredded lettuce
½ cup shredded cheddar cheese
½ cup salsa
8 hard taco shells

1. In a large skillet, brown the ground beef. Drain the excess fat from the ground beef.
2. Add the taco seasoning and water. Stir well.
3. Put the ground beef mixture into a serving bowl.
4. Put the chopped tomato, shredded lettuce, shredded cheese, and salsa in separate serving bowls.
5. Serve with the ground beef and taco shells.

Have your dinner guests each make their own creations using whatever ingredients they choose.

While cooking, children must be supervised by a responsible adult at all times.

The **ABC**s of Kitchen Safety and Fun . . .
Never put electric appliances in the sink.

Nostalgic Meatloaf

Almost like grandma's, but a lot easier to make.

▶ Difficulty: Medium

Makes 6 servings

1 pound ground beef
1 egg, beaten
¾ cup spaghetti sauce
1 cup seasoned bread crumbs
½ tsp. salt
¼ tsp. pepper

1. Preheat the oven to 350 degrees.
2. Spray the baking pan with cooking spray.
3. In a large bowl, combine all ingredients.
4. Shape meat mixture into a meat loaf and place it into the prepared pan.
5. Bake for 50–60 minutes, or until meatloaf is fully cooked.

Let the meatloaf sit for about 5–10 minutes before you slice and serve it, so it has time to set. For side dishes, consider serving Parmesan Potato Fries (page 79) or Old-Fashioned Mashed Potatoes (page 80), as well as a salad or fresh vegetables.

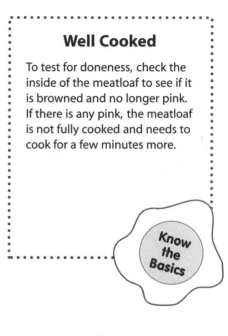

Well Cooked

To test for doneness, check the inside of the meatloaf to see if it is browned and no longer pink. If there is any pink, the meatloaf is not fully cooked and needs to cook for a few minutes more.

Know the Basics

Healthy Habits

Be sure to wash your hands with soap and water before touching food. It is also important to wash your hands after handling raw meat or fish, before you start touching other things.

Orange Chicken

If you don't like onions, just take them off the chicken before serving.

▶ Difficulty: Hard

Makes 4 servings

4 skinless, boneless chicken breasts
4 tsp. Dijon-flavored mustard
2 green onions, chopped
¾ cup orange juice
2 tsp. butter or margarine
3 Tbsp. brown sugar

1. Preheat the oven to 350 degrees.
2. Place the chicken into a 9" × 13" baking dish.
3. Spread the mustard and onion pieces evenly over the chicken breasts.
4. Pour the orange juice into the dish around and over the chicken. (No **basting** required.)
5. Top each chicken breast with dots of butter and sprinkle with the brown sugar.
6. Bake, uncovered, for 30–35 minutes, or until chicken is fully cooked.

For delicious side dishes, look at Fruity Rice (page 82), Sweetened Baby Carrots (page 84), or Green Beans with Almonds (page 85).

Cook It Through

To test for doneness, cut into the chicken and see if the chicken is white on the inside. If there is any pink, the chicken is not fully cooked and needs to cook for a few minutes more.

Know the Basics

basting: to moisten at intervals with a liquid (such as melted butter or pan drippings) during cooking

Zesty Chicken

Tasty and crispy served plain, or as a sandwich with lettuce and tomatoes.

▶ Difficulty: Medium

While cooking, children must be supervised by a responsible adult at all times.

Makes 4 servings

4 boneless, skinless chicken breasts
2 Tbsp. mayonnaise
¾ cup seasoned bread crumbs
2 Tbsp. grated Parmesan cheese

1. Preheat the oven to 400 degrees.
2. Spray the baking pan with cooking spray.
3. Lay the chicken breast fillets in the baking pan. (If you want your chicken breast fillets to be flatter, pound them with a meat mallet before putting them in the baking pan.)
4. Spread a thin layer of mayonnaise over each chicken breast.
5. Sprinkle the bread crumbs and the Parmesan cheese over the chicken.
6. Bake for 20–25 minutes, or until the chicken is crispy and fully cooked.

This chicken is great for an Italian meal, so consider serving it with Spaghetti with Tomato Sauce (page 75), and Cheesy Garlic Bread (page 87).

Cooking Food

When cooking, make sure the food is fully cooked throughout before serving and eating it. Avoid rare foods. Hamburger, poultry, and pork should not be pink in color when they are cut open.

Crispy, Crunchy Chicken Legs

These make a great dinner, and the leftovers make a great lunch for school, even cold.

▶ Difficulty: Medium

Create Crumbs

You can buy ready-made corn flake crumbs or make your own by putting corn flakes in a resealable bag and smashing them with a rolling pin or meat mallet until they are all crumbs.

Makes 4 chicken legs

1 cup corn flake crumbs
1 Tbsp. flour
½ tsp. paprika
½ tsp. salt
¼ tsp. pepper
½ cup milk
4 chicken legs

WORDS to KNOW

pie plate: Shallow dish made of glass or metal, used for making pies

1. Preheat the oven to 375 degrees.
2. In one flat **pie plate**, pour the milk.
3. In another flat pie plate or shallow bowl, combine the corn flake crumbs with flour and spices.
4. Roll the chicken legs first in the milk and then in the crumbs to coat them well.
5. Place chicken legs into a baking pan.
6. Bake for 35–45 minutes, or until the chicken legs are fully cooked.

If you're having a nice meal with your family or company, Sweet Potato Casserole (page 81) will be an excellent side dish.

What's for Dinner?

Parmesan Chicken Fingers

This simple dish is just like store-bought and fast food chicken fingers, only better for you.

▶ Difficulty: Hard

Just Right

To test for doneness, cut open one of the chicken fingers to make sure the chicken is white on the inside. If there is any pink, the chicken is not fully cooked and needs to cook for a few minutes more.

Know the Basics

Makes 4 servings

2 boneless, skinless chicken breasts
1 egg, beaten
¼ cup milk
1 Tbsp. oil
1 Tbsp. water
½ cup bread crumbs

¼ cup grated Parmesan cheese
2 Tbsp. flour
½ tsp. salt
¼ tsp. pepper
2 Tbsp. oil

1. Cut the chicken breasts into slices or chunks, and set aside in a large bowl.
2. In a small bowl, combine the beaten egg, milk, 1 Tbsp. of oil, and water.
3. Pour over the chicken.
4. In a flat pie plate, combine the bread crumbs, Parmesan cheese, flour, salt, and pepper. Mix together.
5. Remove the chicken fingers from the liquid mixture and dip into the bread crumb mixture, coating evenly.
6. Set the chicken fingers out onto a plate or a sheet of waxed paper.
7. In a large skillet, heat 2 Tbsp. of oil.
8. Cook the chicken fingers in the hot oil until they are lightly browned, turning and flipping chicken fingers as necessary until they are fully cooked.

For a Saturday lunch or an easy dinner, have a bowl of Tasty Tomato Soup (page 59) or Creamy Corn Chowder (page 57).

Cheese-Encrusted Fish Fillets

You can use either frozen or fresh fish fillets, depending on what you have in your refrigerator.

▶ Difficulty: Hard

Makes 4 servings

1 pound fish fillets (any type like whitefish, turbot, orange roughy)
1 (4-ounce) package softened cream cheese
1 garlic clove, minced
2 green onions, chopped
1 tsp. lemon juice
1 Tbsp. chopped parsley

1. Preheat oven to 350 degrees. Spray a 9" × 13" baking pan with cooking spray.
2. Lay the fish fillets in a single layer in the baking pan.
3. In a small bowl, combine the cream cheese, garlic, green onions, and lemon juice. Mix well.
4. Spread the cream cheese mixture over the top of each fish fillet.
5. Bake for 35–40 minutes, or until the fish is lightly browned on top and it is fully cooked.

Sprinkle with parsley before serving. For side dishes, try Green Beans with Almonds (page 85) or a Classic Caesar Salad (page 88).

Test Baked Fish for Doneness

With a fork, pick off a piece from the end of the fish when you think it might be done cooking. If the fish flakes off easily, it is done. If it doesn't come off easily, cook it for a few minutes longer and repeat the process.

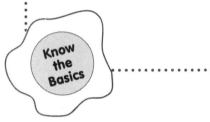

Know the Basics

Did You Know...

Food Trivia

The world has over 30,000 kinds of fish in the earth's waters.

Oven-Fried Fish

If you are a fan of frozen, breaded fish fillets, here's an option that is just as easy to make, and a whole lot healthier, too.

▶ Difficulty: Medium

The **ABC**s of Kitchen Safety and Fun . . .

Oven mitts are a must when touching hot things.

Makes 4 servings

1 pound fish fillets (any type like whitefish, turbot, orange roughy)
½ cup milk
½ cup seasoned bread crumbs
2 Tbsp. grated Parmesan cheese

1. Preheat oven to 350 degrees. Spray a 9" × 13" baking pan with cooking spray.
2. Put the milk in a flat pie plate or shallow bowl.
3. In another flat pie plate, combine the bread crumbs and Parmesan cheese.
4. Dip the fish into the milk and then into the bread crumb mixture.
5. Place the fish into the prepared baking pan.
6. Bake for 20–25 minutes, or until fully cooked.

If you serve the fish on buns, with lettuce and tomatoes, Parmesan Potato Fries (page 79) will go well.

What did the circus lion say as he ate the clown?

"Gee, this food tastes funny!"

Tuna Noodle Casserole

This classic is an old, familiar "comfort food." It makes you feel so good when you eat it, and the leftovers taste as good as the original meal.

▶ Difficulty: Medium

Makes 6–8 servings

8 ounces egg noodles
1 (10¾-ounce) can cream of mushroom soup
1 cup milk
2 (6-ounce) cans tuna fish, packed in water, drained
¼ cup fried onions, for topping

1. Preheat the oven to 375 degrees. Spray a 2-quart casserole dish with cooking spray.
2. Prepare the egg noodles according to package directions. Drain.
3. In large bowl, combine the cooked noodles, mushroom soup, milk, and drained tuna. Mix well.
4. Pour the tuna noodle mixture into the prepared casserole dish. Sprinkle the top of the casserole with fried onions.
5. Bake for 25–30 minutes. (If the onions start to get too brown, cover the casserole dish until it is done cooking.)

Let the casserole dish cool slightly before serving with warm rolls or Cheesy Garlic Bread (page 87).

The **ABCs** of Kitchen Safety and Fun . . .

Put everything away when you are done.

Play It Safe

Don't overfill pots and pans. If they overflow while you are cooking, you will definitely end up with a mess, and you might get splattered or splashed with hot liquids.

Spaghetti with Tomato Sauce (Homemade!)

Everyone will be so impressed that you made this one from scratch.

▶ Difficulty: Hard

While cooking, children must be supervised by a responsible adult at all times.

Makes 6 servings

1 pound spaghetti noodles	1 tsp. dried basil
1 tsp. oil	1 tsp. dried oregano
2 tsp. crushed garlic	¼ tsp. salt
1 (20-ounce) can tomato sauce	¼ tsp. pepper
1 (6-ounce) can tomato paste	2 Tbsp. Parmesan cheese
½ cup water	

1. In a large saucepan, heat the oil over medium heat.

2. Add the garlic. Cook for about 1 minute.

3. Add the tomato sauce and paste, water, basil, oregano, salt, and pepper. Mix well.

4. Increase the heat to high and bring to a boil.

5. While you wait for the sauce to boil, start your spaghetti (or other pasta) according to the package directions.

6. Once the mixture begins to boil, reduce the heat to a simmer, and cook for about 5–10 minutes.

7. Turn the sauce to low while you finish cooking the spaghetti.

8. Drain the spaghetti and serve on plates or in pasta bowls. Pour the sauce over each serving.

Top with Parmesan cheese, if desired, and serve with Classic Caesar Salad (page 88), or Cheesy Garlic Bread (page 87).

Stuffed Shells

You can use manicotti noodles in place of shells, but they may
be difficult to stuff.

▶ Difficulty: Hard

Makes 6 servings

6 ounces jumbo pasta shells
2 cups pasta or spaghetti
   sauce, divided into ½ cup
   and 1½ cup portions
1 egg, lightly beaten

1 (15–16-ounce) container
   ricotta cheese
1 Tbsp. parsley
¼ tsp. salt
¼ tsp. pepper

½ cup grated Parmesan cheese
1½ cups shredded
   mozzarella cheese,
   divided into 1 cup and ½
   cup portions

1. Preheat the oven to 350 degrees.
2. Prepare the shells according to package directions. (Do not overcook the shells because they
   will be too soft to stuff. You can even slightly undercook them by 1–2 minutes.) Drain and cool.
3. Spread ½ cup of the pasta sauce into the bottom of a 9" × 13" baking pan.
4. In a large bowl, combine the beaten egg, ricotta cheese, parsley, salt, pepper, Parmesan
   cheese, and 1 cup of the mozzarella cheese. Mix well.
5. Take a shell and stuff it with the cheese mixture, then lay the shell on top of the pasta sauce,
   cheese side up, in the baking pan.
6. Continue stuffing the remaining shells until you run out of shells (or cheese mixture).
7. Pour the remaining pasta sauce over the shells. Top with the remaining mozzarella cheese.
8. Bake for 25–25 minutes, or until the cheese is melted and lightly browned. (If the cheese
   begins to brown too quickly, cover the pan with a sheet of aluminum foil. This will keep the top
   from cooking too fast.)

If you have leftovers, heat them in the microwave with a little extra sauce to keep the pasta
from getting rubbery.

Baked Ziti

Here's a 30-minute meal the whole family will love.

▶ Difficulty: Hard

Makes 8 servings

1 (16-ounce) package ziti
    noodles
1 onion, chopped
2 tsp. chopped garlic
1 (16-ounce) jar pasta sauce
    (or you can use
    homemade sauce)

1 tsp. dried oregano
1 tsp. dried basil
1 cup shredded mozzarella
    cheese

The **ABCs** of
Kitchen Safety and Fun . . .
Quickly clean up all spills.

1. Prepare the ziti noodles according to package directions. Drain.
2. Preheat the oven to 350 degrees.
3. In a large skillet over medium heat, sauté the onion and garlic.
4. Add the pasta sauce, oregano, and basil.
5. Toss with the drained ziti.
6. Add ½ of the mozzarella cheese. Stir.
7. Pour the ziti mixture into a 9" × 13" baking dish or 2-quart casserole dish.
8. Sprinkle remaining cheese over the top of the casserole. Cover with lid or aluminum foil.
9. Bake for 20–25 minutes, or until the ziti is well heated and the cheese is melted.

Let the casserole stand for about 5 minutes or so before serving with a fresh salad, bread, or even Zesty Chicken (page 69).

Lots of Lasagna

Luckily, lasagna is a big dish that will feed several people—it's always a family favorite!

▶ Difficulty: Hard

Makes 12 servings

1 pound ground beef
1 (28-ounce) jar pasta sauce, any flavor
1 (2-pound) container ricotta cheese
2 cups shredded mozzarella cheese, divided into 1½ cups and ½ cup portions
½ cup grated Parmesan cheese
2 eggs
½ pound (½ box) package no-boil or regular lasagna noodles

1. Preheat the oven to 375 degrees.
2. In a large skillet, brown the ground beef over medium heat. Drain the extra fat from the ground beef.
3. Pour the pasta sauce into the ground beef and mix well. Set aside.
4. In a large bowl, combine the ricotta cheese, 1½ cups of the mozzarella cheese, Parmesan cheese, and eggs. Mix well.
5. In a 9" × 13" baking pan, place 4 uncooked lasagna noodles across the bottom of the pan.
6. Spread about ½ cup of the cheese mixture evenly over the lasagna noodles and top with about ½ cup of the ground beef mixture.
7. Repeat layers with the lasagna noodles, cheese mixture, and ground beef mixture until all the ingredients are used up, ending with the ground beef layer.
8. Top the lasagna with the ½ cup of reserved mozzarella cheese.
9. Cover the pan with a sheet of aluminum foil, and bake 1 hour.
10. Remove the foil and bake an additional 10 minutes (until cheese on top just starts to brown).

Let the lasagna cool for about 10 minutes before serving with fresh salad and Cheesy Garlic Bread (page 87).

Parmesan Potato Fries

You can prepare these potatoes with or without the skin, and in whatever shape you like.

▶ Difficulty: Hard

The **ABC**s of Kitchen Safety and Fun . . .

Review safety rules.

Makes 4 servings

4 potatoes	½ tsp. pepper
2 Tbsp. oil	1 Tbsp. Parmesan cheese
1 tsp. salt	

1. Preheat the oven to 350 degrees. Spray a baking pan or cookie sheet with cooking spray.

2. Wash the potatoes, and cut them into strips or rounds, or any shape you choose.

3. Put the potatoes into a resealable bag or a large bowl.

4. Add the oil to the bag or bowl and mix together until the potatoes are well coated.

5. Sprinkle the potatoes with salt, pepper, and Parmesan cheese. Toss again.

6. Place the potatoes in a single layer onto prepared baking pan or cookie sheet.

7. Bake for 45–50 minutes, or until the potatoes are crispy and golden brown. Halfway through baking, flip the potatoes over so they cook evenly on all sides.

Fried potatoes are good for any casual meal, like the Zesty Chicken on a bun (page 69) or Oven Fried Fish (page 73).

What do you get when a football team plays in your potato field?

Mashed potatoes!

Old-Fashioned Mashed Potatoes

For an extra smooth taste, add a little sour cream to your mashed potatoes before serving.

▶ Difficulty: Hard

Makes 4 servings

4 large potatoes, peeled
½ cup milk

2 Tbsp. butter or margarine
½ tsp. salt

1. Use a vegetable peeler to peel the skin off of the potatoes.
2. Cut each potato into chunks about 1" in size and place them into a large saucepan filled with just enough water to cover the potatoes.
3. Put the saucepan on high heat until the water boils. (Keep an eye on the pan, in case it starts to boil over.)
4. Lower the heat to medium and cook for about 20 minutes, or until the potatoes are tender.
5. Drain the water from the potatoes and put the potatoes back into the saucepan.
6. Use a potato masher to mash the potatoes until they are smooth. (Try not to mash too much or else the potatoes will get too pasty.)
7. Stir in the milk, butter, and salt.

Mashed potatoes are the perfect side dish for many "meat and potatoes" meals, including Crispy Crunchy Chicken Legs (page 70) and Nostalgic Meatloaf (page 67).

Sweet Potato Casserole

Here's a simple, and fancy, side dish that goes very well with chicken or fish.

▶ Difficulty: Medium

> ## Know Your Tools
>
> ***Know how to use the various appliances and utensils you will need.*** If you need to, ask an adult to teach or remind you, especially if you are using anything with hot oil (like a wok), or sharp moving parts (like a food processor).

Makes 6 servings

1½ cups mini marshmallows, divided into 1 cup and ½ cup portions

2 (17-ounce) cans sweet potatoes, drained and mashed

¼ cup margarine, melted

¼ cup orange juice

½ tsp. cinnamon

1. Preheat the oven to 350 degrees.
2. In a large bowl, mash the drained sweet potatoes until they are mostly smooth.
3. Add all the remaining ingredients, with 1 cup of the marshmallows, and gently mix them together.
4. Pour the mixture into a 1-quart casserole dish.
5. Bake 20 minutes.
6. Sprinkle the remaining marshmallows over the top of the casserole, and return to the oven for 5 minutes longer.

Serve this warm, sweet side dish as a special treat at any holiday meal.

The **ABCs** of Kitchen Safety and Fun . . .

Store food properly.

Did You Know...

Food Trivia

Cranberries, a traditional Thanksgiving food, were part of the Pilgrims' feast at the first Thanksgiving in 1621.

While cooking, children must be supervised by a responsible adult at all times.

Fruity Rice

Try this sweet side dish with chicken, fish, or pork. It will jazz up any meal.

▶ Difficulty: Hard

Makes 4 servings

1 cup cooked rice
2 red apples
1 Tbsp. oil
¼ cup raisins
¼ cup dried cranberries

1. Cook the rice according to package directions. Set aside.
2. Chop the apple into small pieces, leaving the skin on.
3. In a small skillet, heat the oil.
4. Add the apples and cook about 5 minutes.
5. Stir in the raisins, dried cranberries, and rice.
6. Continue cooking and stirring until the rice mixture is heated throughout.

The apples and cranberries in this rice make it a nice autumn dish to go with something salty, like ham, or something sweeter, like Orange Chicken (page 68).

Chinese Fried Rice

If you'd like a heartier rice, you can add some leftover chicken, shrimp, or tofu to make this dish a meal all by itself.

▶ Difficulty: Hard

While cooking, children must be supervised by a responsible adult at all times

Makes 4–6 servings

¼ cup oil
1 small onion, chopped
2 cloves garlic, chopped
¼ tsp. ground ginger
½ cup chopped carrots

1 zucchini, sliced
½ cup frozen peas
2 eggs, beaten
2 cups cooked white rice
¼ cup soy sauce

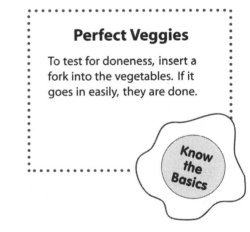

Perfect Veggies

To test for doneness, insert a fork into the vegetables. If it goes in easily, they are done.

Know the Basics

1. Cook the rice according to package directions. Set aside.
2. In a large skillet, heat oil.
3. Add the onion, garlic, ginger, carrots, zucchini, and peas.
4. Cook until the vegetables are tender, about 5 minutes.
5. Remove the skillet from the heat, and put the vegetable mixture into a large bowl.
6. Add the beaten eggs to the skillet, and cook the eggs until they are scrambled.
7. Set the egg mixture aside, in the bowl with the mixed vegetables.
8. Put the cooked rice into the skillet, and stir while reheating.
9. Add the soy sauce to the rice, and add the vegetable and egg mixture back into the skillet with the rice.
10. Stir with the spatula until everything is heated through.

Because this fried rice has eggs and vegetables, it is a good vegetarian meal all by itself. Fried rice is also a great way to use up leftover rice and vegetables.

While cooking, children must be supervised by a responsible adult at all times.

Sweetened Baby Carrots

A quick and colorful side dish that adds variety to any meal.

▶ Difficulty: Medium

Makes 4 servings

1 pound baby carrots
1 Tbsp. butter or margarine
2 Tbsp. brown sugar

1. In a large saucepan, combine the carrots and just enough water to cover them.
2. Put the saucepan over high heat until the water begins to boil.
3. Reduce the heat to medium and continue cooking until the carrots are slightly tender, about 15 minutes.
4. Using a colander, drain the carrots and return them to the saucepan.
5. Add the butter and brown sugar to the saucepan, stirring until the butter is melted and the carrots are well coated.

Like Sweet Potato Casserole (page 81), this sweet treat works best on special occasions, like holidays.

Cooking Carrots

To test for doneness, insert a fork into the carrots. If the fork goes in easily, they are done.

Know the Basics

The **ABCs** of Kitchen Safety and Fun . . . **T**ie long hair back.

Green Beans with Almonds

There's nothing like the fresh, crisp sound of snapping beans. This recipe is not only fun and easy to make, but crunchy and healthy to eat.

▶ Difficulty: Medium

The **ABC**s of Kitchen Safety and Fun . . . **U**nderstand cooking methods.

Makes 4 servings

½ pound fresh green beans
1 Tbsp. butter or margarine
¼ cup slivered almonds
½ tsp. salt
¼ tsp. pepper

1. Trim the beans by snapping off the ends and removing any loose strings, then use a colander to hold the beans while you wash them in cool water.
2. In a large saucepan, heat 2 quarts of water to boiling.
3. Add the beans to the boiling water, and cook them for about 5 minutes until they are slightly tender, but still crisp.
4. Drain the green beans and return them to the saucepan.
5. Add the butter, almonds, salt, and pepper, and toss them until the butter is melted and evenly coating the green beans.

Fresh beans are a simple side dish for any meal, and their bright color goes well with lighter foods, like chicken and fish.

Kid: Why is my sandwich full of holes?

Mom: Because I used hole-wheat bread!

Food Trivia

Hush Puppies, a great traditional food from the South, got its name when pieces of fried cornmeal batter were fed to dogs that begged for food. Owners would then say, "now hush puppy."

Down-Home Cornbread

Cornbread is an old favorite, and still *soooo* good!

▶ Difficulty: Medium

Makes 16 pieces of cornbread

¾ cup cornmeal
1½ cups flour
1 cup sugar
2 Tbsp. milk
1 Tbsp. baking powder

½ tsp. salt
1 egg
½ cup warm water
4 Tbsp. butter, melted

1. Preheat the oven to 400 degrees. Spray an 8"-square pan with cooking spray.
2. In a large bowl, combine the cornmeal, flour, sugar, milk, baking powder, and salt.
3. In another bowl, beat the egg.
4. Add the water and melted butter to the egg, and mix well.
5. Combine the two mixtures and blend together.
6. Pour the cornbread batter into the prepared baking pan, using a rubber spatula to clear the batter from the bowl.
7. Bake 20–25 minutes, or until golden brown.

The mild taste of cornbread goes very well with creamy but flavorful soup like Tasty Tomato Soup (page 59), or Chili in No Time (page 61).

Cheesy Garlic Bread

Garlic bread is a nice appetizer, but it's especially delicious served with saucy Italian food. Yum!

▶ Difficulty: Hard

Makes 8 servings

1 large loaf soft Italian bread
½ cup oil
½ cup (1 stick) butter

3 large garlic cloves, peeled and finely chopped, or 1½ Tbsp. minced garlic from a jar
½ cup Parmesan cheese

1. Preheat the oven to 400 degrees.
2. Slice the bread in half lengthwise, and lay it out on a large piece of aluminum foil spread over a cookie sheet. (Make sure your piece of foil is large enough to wrap around the bread during baking.)
3. In a small saucepan over low heat, combine the oil, butter, and garlic, stirring until the butter is melted.
4. Use a pastry brush to spread the butter coating over both halves of the bread.
5. Sprinkle Parmesan cheese over the top.
6. Leaving the loaf open, bring the foil up and over the sides and top of the bread, so it is covered.
7. Bake 10–12 minutes. (If you want to crisp up the top, open up the foil and bake 5 minutes more.)

As tasty as it is, Cheesy Garlic Bread can't be a meal by itself—but you can serve it with Lots of Lasagna (page 78), Stuffed Shells (page 76), or any other saucy and delicious main dish.

The **ABCs** of Kitchen Safety and Fun . . .

Value the time you spend with your family.

What is the difference between a moldy bowl of lettuce and a depressing song?

One is a bad salad, and the other is a sad ballad!

Classic Caesar Salad

Add some Parmesan Chicken Fingers to this salad for a tasty Chicken Caesar that the entire family will enjoy.

▶ Difficulty: Easy

Makes 2 servings

1 small bunch romaine lettuce, or about 2 cups torn up
2 Tbsp. freshly shredded Parmesan cheese
½ cup croutons
2 Tbsp. bottled Caesar salad dressing

1. Wash the romaine lettuce.
2. Tear the lettuce into small pieces and place it into a large bowl.
3. Top with Parmesan cheese and croutons.
4. Using serving utensils, toss salad dressing into the salad and serve immediately.

Caesar salad is light and fresh, and in addition to being a meal by itself, it goes very well with simple dinners, like grilled steak, or Italian foods like Baked Ziti (page 77).

Fancy Fruit Salad

The best thing about fruit salad is that you can always choose different fruit based on your favorites, or what's fresh for the season.

▶ Difficulty: Medium

Makes 6 servings

½ cup grapes (red, green, or a combination of both)
½ cup sliced strawberries
2 bananas, sliced
½ cantaloupe, cut into chunks
½ cup orange juice
½ cup shredded coconut

1. In a large bowl, combine all of the fruit.
2. Stir the orange juice and coconut into the fruit, and toss well.

Serve immediately, as a brunch or lunch side dish with Cheesy Scrambled Eggs (page 26) or Breakfast Crepes (page 19).

Get a Head Start

It's okay to make the fruit salad in advance. Just wait to add the bananas until you're ready to serve.

Tip

Did You Know...

Food Trivia

Orange juice and lemon juice contain an acid that helps keep fruit, like apples and bananas, from turning brown after they are cut open.

Waldorf Salad

This salad was named after the Waldorf Astoria Hotel in New York City where it was first made. Now there are so many versions of it, it has become a famous-named salad.

▶ Difficulty: Medium

Makes 4 servings

1 large red apple, chopped
2 stalks celery, chopped
2 Tbsp. raisins
1 tsp. lemon juice
2 Tbsp. chopped nuts
2 Tbsp. mayonnaise

1. Chop the apple, celery, and nuts into ½" chunks. (If you don't have an apple corer, ask an adult to help you get the stem and seeds out of the apple.)
2. In a large bowl, combine all of the ingredients, and mix well.
3. Keep the salad refrigerated until you are ready to serve.

Waldorf salad is another special treat, perfect as a first course for holiday meals.

Play It Safe

Storing Food: Keep hot foods hot and cold foods cold. Do not leave cooked food out at room temperature for more than one hour. When picnicking, be sure to keep cold food in a cooler at cool temperatures, and keep all food away from the sunlight.

The **ABC**s of Kitchen Safety and Fun . . .

Wash your hands before you touch food.

Chapter 7

Desserts and Special Treats

ometimes, even when dinner has been delicious, you might make extra room just to have a taste of dessert. Once you are the cook, you'll notice that everyone else is making room for your creations!

The desserts here are a lot of fun to make and share as a special treat after a meal. Make some for home, or for special people like your grandparents, teachers, or friends. You will be so proud of yourself!

Who's Who?

Nicky had a great time decorating these gingerbread cookies. Can you tell which two are EXACTLY alike?

Double Chocolate Chip Cookies

These chewy sensations satisfy any chocolate **craving,** and are especially good with a glass of cold milk.

▶ Difficulty: Medium

Makes 2½ dozen cookies

½ cup sugar
½ cup brown sugar
½ cup butter or margarine, softened
2 eggs
½ tsp. vanilla

1¾ cup flour
¼ cup unsweetened cocoa powder
1 tsp. baking soda
¼ tsp. salt
1 cup chocolate chips

1. Preheat the oven to 375 degrees.
2. In a large mixing bowl using an electric mixer, combine sugar, brown sugar, margarine, eggs, and vanilla. Mix well until the batter is smooth.
3. Add the remaining ingredients, except for the chocolate chips.
4. When the batter is smooth and creamy, stir in the chocolate chips.
5. Drop dough by tablespoonfuls onto a cookie sheet.
6. Bake for 8–10 minutes, until golden.
7. Remove cookie sheet from the oven and let it cool 1 minute before removing the cookies.

Store cookies in a tin lined with waxed paper, or freeze them in an airtight container to serve at another time.

Crack an Egg

Gently crack the eggshell on the edge of a cup or bowl; let the shell crack into two parts and, holding on to the shell, let the egg drop easily into the bowl. It's always best to crack an egg on the edge of a clear glass cup (like a glass measuring cup) or small glass bowl, and drop the yolk and white into the cup or bowl before putting it together with other ingredients. That way, if the cracked egg has any eggshell in it, or if it is a bad egg that has blood or a red spot in it, you can throw it away before it ruins your other ingredients.

Know the Basics

Bake 'em Your Way

Bake the cookies for 8 minutes for chewy cookies, and longer (up to 10 minutes) for crispier ones.

Tip

Little Lemon Squares

Tart and tangy, these cookie squares are simple, and yet a favorite for many people.

▶ Difficulty: Medium

Makes about 2 dozen squares

1½ cups flour
⅔ cup oil
½ cup powdered sugar
2 Tbsp. lemon juice

3 eggs
1½ cups sugar
½ cup flour

1. Preheat the oven to 350 degrees. Spray a 9"-square baking pan with cooking spray.
2. In a large bowl, combine the 1½ cups flour, oil, and powdered sugar.
3. Pour the mixture into the prepared pan and, with your fingers, flatten the crust around the bottoms and sides of the pan.
4. Bake the crust for 18–20 minutes, or until it is lightly browned.
5. In a large bowl, combine the remaining ingredients.
6. Pour the filling mixture into the crust, and bake an additional 20–25 minutes, or until the mixture is cooked throughout.
7. Cool and cut into 1"–1½" squares.

Lemon squares are the perfect dessert for people who are allergic to (or don't like) chocolate.

Just So You Know

The center for the lemon squares will be somewhat soft when fully cooked. Once they cool, they will become firmer, but remain chewy.

Tip

Dad: The crust on that apple pie was awful tough.

Tad: That wasn't the crust—you ate the paper plate!

Trail Mix Cookies

Just like a trail mix, almost any combination will work in these cookies. Try different versions depending upon what you like.

▶ Difficulty: Medium

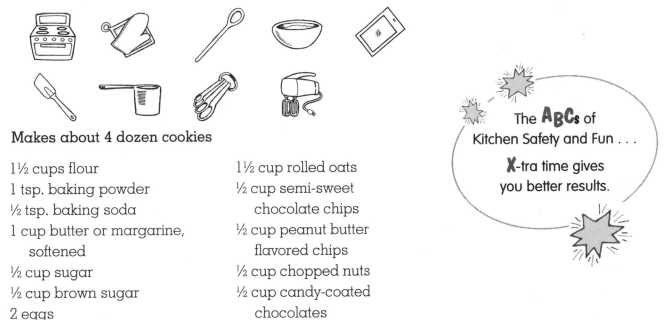

Makes about 4 dozen cookies

1½ cups flour
1 tsp. baking powder
½ tsp. baking soda
1 cup butter or margarine, softened
½ cup sugar
½ cup brown sugar
2 eggs
1 tsp. vanilla

1½ cup rolled oats
½ cup semi-sweet chocolate chips
½ cup peanut butter flavored chips
½ cup chopped nuts
½ cup candy-coated chocolates

The **ABC**s of Kitchen Safety and Fun . . .

X-tra time gives you better results.

1. Preheat the oven to 350 degrees.
2. In a large bowl, combine the flour, baking powder, and baking soda. Set aside.
3. In a large mixing bowl, use an electric mixer to cream together the butter, sugar, brown sugar, and eggs.
4. Add in the vanilla, and mix again.
5. Gradually combine the flour mixture with the butter mixture, and continue mixing.
6. Add in the remaining ingredients, one at a time, stirring as you add each one.
7. Drop the dough by tablespoonfuls onto a cookie sheet.
8. Bake for 8–10 minutes, or until the cookies are lightly browned.

Like Double Chocolate Chip Cookies (page 93), you can make and freeze these cookies in advance, and bring them for dessert when you have dinner at someone else's house.

Graham Ice Cream Sandwiches

These yummy (and easy!) treats are a perfect treat for a summer day.

▶ Difficulty: Easy

Makes 2 ice cream sandwiches

4 graham cracker squares
½ cup ice cream, sherbet, or frozen yogurt of your choice, slightly softened
Candy sprinkles, optional

1. Place ¼ cup ice cream on one graham cracker square, and top with a second to make a "sandwich."
2. Dip the edges of the "sandwich" in candy sprinkles, mini-chips, or nuts for an extra fun snack.

Eat your ice cream sandwich right away, or wrap it in plastic wrap and freeze until you are ready to eat it.

Food Trivia

People have been eating ice cream around the world for over 4,000 years, but only in the United States since the 1800s.

Healthy Habits

Be sure to wash hands with soap and water before touching food. It is also important to wash your hands after handling raw meat or fish, before you start touching other things.

The **ABCs** of Kitchen Safety and Fun . . . **Y**ou can learn a lot!

Cocoa Balls

Rolling the dough to make these tasty cookies can be fun for the entire family!

▶ Difficulty: Hard

While cooking, children must be supervised by a responsible adult at all times.

Makes about 4 dozen cocoa balls

Dough
1 cup (2 sticks) butter or
   margarine, softened
2 ounces unsweetened
   chocolate squares, melted
   and slightly cooled

¾ cup confectioners' sugar
1 egg yolk
1½ tsp. vanilla
2 cups flour
½ tsp. salt
½ cup chopped walnuts, optional

Coating
¾ cup confectioners' sugar
3 Tbsp. unsweetened cocoa

1. In a small pan over low heat, melt the chocolate squares
2. In a large bowl using an electric mixer, combine the butter, melted chocolate, confectioners' sugar, egg yolk, and vanilla. Mix until well blended.
3. Add the flour and salt. Mix until smooth.
4. Add walnuts, if desired.
5. Cover the dough and put it in the refrigerator for at least 1–2 hours, until the dough is firm enough to roll into balls.
6. Preheat the oven to 350 degrees.
7. Use a tablespoon to scoop up the dough and roll it into a ball, about 1" in size.
8. Put balls on an ungreased cookie sheet, leaving about 2" between each cookie.
9. Bake 10–12 minutes. Remove cookies from the cookie sheet and cool about 10 minutes.
10. In a medium bowl, mix together the coating ingredients.
11. Roll slightly cooled cookies in sugar-cocoa coating.

These cookies are extra rich, but make a great addition to a dessert buffet during parties or holidays.

Food Trivia

Ice cream sundaes were first only available on Sundays. The spelling was changed from Sunday to sundae to respect the Lord's day.

Banana Split Ice Cream Pie

Here's an extra-special treat to make for dessert.

▶ Difficulty: Medium

Makes 1 pie and about 8 servings

1 (6-ounce) ready-to-use graham cracker or chocolate piecrust
2 bananas
1 quart vanilla ice cream, softened
½ cup hot fudge sauce
Whipped cream
Maraschino cherries
Chopped nuts, optional

1. Slice bananas and lay them out in the bottom of the piecrust.
2. Scoop out the softened ice cream and spread it evenly over the bananas.
3. Freeze the pie for at least 2 hours to harden the ice cream.
4. Let the pie sit out for about 5 minutes prior to serving so it is easier to cut.

What's better than ice cream after a cookout? Set out the fudge, whipped cream, cherries, and nuts so each person can top their own slice of pie.

Cut the Cake

How would you cut a round cake into nine pieces with only four cuts of the knife?

Thumbprint Surprise

Try different flavors of fruit **preserves** to make these cookies more colorful.

▶ Difficulty: Medium

WORDS to KNOW

preserves—Fruit that is canned, or made into jams or jellies for future use

Makes about 4 dozen thumbprint surprises

1 cup (2 sticks) butter or
   margarine, softened
½ cup brown sugar
1 egg
1 tsp. vanilla
3 cups flour

½ tsp. salt
About ½ cup sugar, set aside
   on a small plate or saucer
½ cup jelly, jam, or preserves,
   any flavor of your choice

1. Preheat the oven to 350 degrees.
2. In large mixing bowl, using an electric mixer, cream the butter and brown sugar until smooth.
3. Add the egg and vanilla, and mix together.
4. Gradually mix in the flour and salt, stirring with a spoon as the batter becomes stiffer.
5. Scoop up about a tablespoon of dough, and roll it into a ball, about 1" in size.
6. Roll the dough in the set-aside sugar to coat the outside of the ball.
7. Put the balls onto an ungreased cookie sheet, leaving about 2" between each cookie.
8. Slightly press down on the ball with your thumb to form a well in the middle.
9. Place about ½ tsp. of jelly into each well.
10. Bake 10–12 minutes until cookies are lightly browned.

These cookies are great any time, but they also make especially good holiday gifts.

Peanut Butter Bites

Try adding chocolate chips to these cookies for an extra burst of flavor.

The **ABC**s of Kitchen Safety and Fun . . .

Zealous cooks will have fun (and eat well!) for a lifetime.

▶ Difficulty: Medium

Makes 3 dozen cookies

1 cup (2 sticks) butter or margarine	2 eggs
¾ cup sugar	2½ cups flour
¾ cup brown sugar	2 tsp. baking soda
¾ cup peanut butter	1 tsp. vanilla
	¼ tsp. salt

1. Preheat the oven to 350 degrees.
2. In a mixing bowl, using an electric mixer, cream together the butter, sugars, peanut butter, vanilla, and eggs.
3. Slowly add the remaining ingredients, and mix well.
4. Use a tablespoon to scoop out the dough and roll the dough into balls with your hands.
5. Place the dough onto a cookie sheet.
6. Flatten each ball out with a spatula or fork, making sure there is about 2" between each cookie.
7. Bake for 8–10 minutes, or until cookies are lightly browned.

Peanut butter cookies are also good for people who can't (or don't) eat chocolate, but keep in mind that some people are allergic to peanuts. For some variety on your dessert table, you can also make Little Lemon Squares (page 94).

What's soft, white, sweet, and comes from Mars?

Martian-mallows!

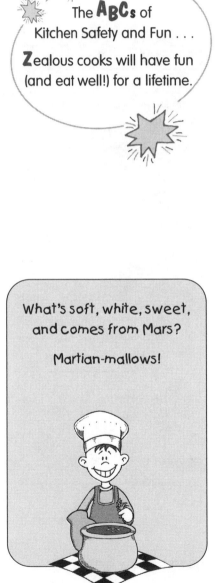

Chewy Gingerbread Cookies

These classic cookies are a favorite of many people, young and old alike.

▶ Difficulty: Medium

Makes 3½ dozen cookies

2 cups flour
1 tsp. baking soda
1 tsp. ground ginger
1 tsp. cinnamon
½ tsp. nutmeg

¼ tsp. salt
1½ sticks butter or margarine,
    softened
1 cup brown sugar
½ cup light molasses

1 egg
2 Tbsp. sugar, to sprinkle on
    tops on cookies

1. Preheat the oven to 350 degrees.
2. In a large bowl, mix together the flour, baking soda, ginger, cinnamon, nutmeg, and salt, and set aside.
3. In a mixing bowl, using an electric mixer, beat together the butter and brown sugar until it is creamy.
4. Add the molasses and the egg.
5. Gradually add the dry ingredients into the batter, and mix together until the batter is smooth.
6. Put the dough into the refrigerator for at least 1 hour.
7. Drop dough by tablespoonfuls onto a cookie sheet, leaving about 2" between each cookie.
8. Flatten each cookie with the back of a spoon or with a spatula, and sprinkle cookies with sugar.
9. Bake for 8–10 minutes, or until the cookies are crinkled and crackly looking.
10. Remove the cookies from the oven, and cool slightly before removing them from the cookie sheet.

These cookies are a great snack for watching a movie at home, or for packing away in your lunch bag.

Chocolate Dipped Surprises

When you dip food in chocolate, the possibilities are endless!
Try fresh or dried fruit, cookies, pretzels, or even licorice sticks.

▶ Difficulty: Easy

½ cup of the melted chocolate will make enough for about
10–12 dipped items

Chocolate melt pellets (found typically in craft stores for candy
    making)
Pretzel rods or rings, fortune cookies, strawberries, or any
    other treat
Candy sprinkles, any color or type, optional
Nuts, finely chopped, optional
Waxed paper

1. In a plastic or glass bowl, heat about ½ cup of the candy
    melts in the microwave for about 1 minute. Stir chocolate to
    make it smooth.
2. Dip the item of choice into the chocolate.
3. Place dipped item onto a waxed paper lined cookie sheet to
    harden. (Once you've filled the sheet, you can place it in the
    refrigerator to help the chocolate harden faster.)
4. Before chocolate hardens, top with candy sprinkles or nuts.

A fondue pot will keep the chocolate melted longer. If you
have one, set it out with a platter of mixed fruit and cookies.
Guests at your dessert buffet can dip their own favorite treats.

Did You Know...

Food Trivia

- The candy bar "Baby Ruth" was named after the daughter of U.S. President Grover Cleveland in 1921.
- Tootsie Rolls were the first wrapped penny candy in America.
- The first bubble gum was introduced in 1906 and was called Blibber Blubber.
- Pez candies were first made as a breath mint.

Favorite Fudge

For a rocky road fudge, add chopped nuts or even mini marshmallows to the fudge before refrigerating.

▶ Difficulty: Medium

Makes 2 dozen pieces

3 cups sugar

1½ sticks butter or margarine

⅔ cup evaporated milk

1 (12-ounce) package chocolate chips

1 (7½-ounce) jar marshmallow cream

1 tsp. vanilla

1. Spray a 9" × 13" pan with cooking spray.

2. In a large saucepan, combine sugar, butter, and milk.

3. Stirring constantly, heat the mixture until it boils (which takes about 5 minutes).

4. Turn off the heat and remove the pan from the burner.

5. Add the chocolate chips, stirring until they melt.

6. Add the remaining ingredients, and stir until the mixture is well blended.

7. Pour the fudge mixture into the prepared pan.

8. Refrigerate until the fudge hardens (at least 4 hours) before cutting.

Fudge also makes a great gift for people like teachers, babysitters, or your best friend's parents.

Did You Know...

Food Trivia

Candy like chocolate, fudge, caramel, and toffee is made from milk and cream.

I tried making a pineapple upside-down cake.

How did it turn out?

It was a complete flop!

World's Best Brownies

You will receive so many compliments for these brownies, because everyone loves them.

▶ Difficulty: Hard

Makes 1½ dozen brownies

1 cup flour
1½ cups sugar
¾ cup unsweetened cocoa
½ cup brown sugar
½ tsp. salt
½ cup (1 stick) butter or
    margarine, melted

3 eggs, lightly beaten
½ tsp. vanilla
¼ cup semi-sweet choco-
    late chips
¼ cup white chocolate chips
½ cup chopped nuts, optional

1. Preheat the oven to 350 degrees. Spray a 9"-square pan with cooking spray.
2. In a large bowl using an electric mixer, combine the flour, sugar, cocoa, brown sugar, and salt.
3. Melt the butter in a small saucepan over low heat.
4. Add the melted butter, eggs, and vanilla to the sugar mixture. Mix well.
5. Fold in the semi-sweet and white chocolate chips, and nuts (if desired).
6. Pour the batter into the prepared pan.
7. Bake for 30–35 minutes, or until done.

Cool before cutting, and serve with cold milk.

Is It Done Yet?

To test for doneness, insert a toothpick into the center of the brownies. If the toothpick comes out clean, the brownies are done. If there is batter on the toothpick, the brownies need to cook another 1–2 minutes. Then, test again with a clean toothpick.

Know the Basics

Did You Know...

Food Trivia

In 1900, sugar sold for $.04/pound. Today it sells for more than 10 times that amount.

Ultimate Peanut Butter Chocolate Squares

You can't go wrong with these peanut butter and chocolate treats. Not only are they easy to make, they are a hit at every gathering.

▶ Difficulty: Medium

Super Scraper

A rubber spatula will be very helpful for getting peanut butter out of the measuring cup, for scraping the batter into the pan, and also for spreading the melted chocolate evenly.

Makes about 3–4 dozen squares

¾ cup graham cracker crumbs

1 cup smooth peanut butter

1 cup (2 sticks) butter or margarine, melted

3½ cups confectioners' (powdered) sugar

1½ cups chocolate chips

1. Spray a 9" × 13" pan with cooking spray. Set aside.
2. In a large bowl, combine the graham cracker crumbs, peanut butter, melted butter, and confectioners' sugar. Mix well.
3. Spread batter out into prepared pan.
4. In a medium saucepan, heat 1 quart of water.
5. Put chocolate chips into a smaller saucepan and set this pan inside the saucepan of water. (By setting the smaller saucepan into the larger saucepan of water, we are creating a double boiler. You can also use a specially designed double boiler, if you have one. This process allows the chocolate chips to melt slowly without being directly on top of the burner.)
6. Continue stirring chocolate chips until they are completely melted.
7. When the chocolate chips are melted, spread the chocolate over the peanut butter mixture.
8. Place pan into the refrigerator to cool before cutting into squares.

The best thing about these treats is that all the bowls are fun to lick!

Rocky Road Pudding Pie

Here is a delicious dessert treat that can be made in only a few minutes. It's so easy to prepare, and so much fun to eat.

▶ Difficulty: Easy

Makes 6 servings

1 (6-ounce) ready-to-use graham cracker or chocolate pie crust
1 (3.9-ounce) package instant chocolate pudding
2 cups cold milk
½ cup mini marshmallows
¼ cup chopped peanuts

1. In a bowl, prepare the pudding according to the package directions.
2. Add the marshmallows and peanuts to pudding, and mix well.
3. Pour the pudding mixture into the piecrust.

Refrigerate until ready to serve. Whipped topping and a light sprinkle of nuts will take this dessert from "fun" to "*fancy!*" Enjoy!

Food Trivia

Rocky Road ice cream was named after the troubled United States during the Great Depression.

Play It Safe

When Buying Food: Check expiration dates to see how long the food will be safe to store and safe to eat. When buying produce or deli foods, make sure they are fresh and have been properly refrigerated in the store. At home, promptly store the foods at their proper temperature.

Chocolate Peanut Butter Pudding

Try chunky peanut butter for a crunchier taste.

▶ Difficulty: Easy

Makes 4 servings

1 (3.9-ounce) package instant chocolate pudding
2 cups cold milk
½ cup peanut butter
¼ cup chopped nuts, optional

1. Prepare the pudding according to the package directions.
2. Use a whisk to stir the peanut butter into the pudding.
3. Pour the pudding into individual serving dishes.
4. Sprinkle with chopped nuts, if desired.

Refrigerate until ready to serve. Add whipped topping, if desired.

Better Yet!

You can also make a rocky road chocolate peanut butter pudding by adding some mini marshmallows, too.

Tip

Mystery Meal #6 _____

1/2 tsp. salt	1/2 tsp. baking soda
1/3 cup oil	2/3 cup sugar
	1 1/2 cups flour
	2 eggs, beaten
	1/2 cup milk
	2 cups fresh blueberries

Can you tell what this recipe will make by reading the list of ingredients? Write the name of the finished food at the top of the card.

What's Cookin' at Your House?

Are you a creative cook? You may decide to experiment with some of these recipes. If you try something new and everyone likes it, make notes here so you remember what you changed. You can also use this space to write down special recipes from your friends or family.

Recipe Title: ....

Makes .... **servings**

Ingredients:

....

....

....

....

....

Directions:

....

....

....

....

....

....

....

....

....

....

....

....

Chapter 8

Smoothies and Beverages

I'm Thirsty

These kids are all thirsty—but everyone wants to drink something different. Crack the code on each glass to figure out who is sipping what. Remember: There's a different code on each glass!

1. 13 - 9 - 12 - 11
2. epos
3.
4. H₂O
5. KVJDF
6.

If you have never made a smoothie or fun beverage at home, now is the time to try it. For some of these drinks, you will need a blender, and most of them taste best in a nice, tall glass.

But those are the only rules! You can use fruit, yogurt, ice cream, milk, juice . . . anything that sounds like it might taste good. (And because they are mostly only one serving, if your concoction isn't so good, you haven't wasted too much in your experiment!)

Smoothies and floats are so easy to make and so delicious. Once you've tried one as a breakfast drink, or after-practice snack, they may just become your next favorite treat!

Creamsicle Shake

You'll go nuts over this creamy shake. You can also freeze it for an extra delightful treat.

▶ Difficulty: Medium

Makes 1 shake

About 1 cup frozen vanilla yogurt or
    ice cream
½ cup orange juice

1. Combine the frozen yogurt and the orange juice in a blender.
2. Put the lid on, and blend for 1 minute, or until smooth.

Serve immediately in a tall, frosty glass.

Play It Safe

Tie back long hair and pull up long sleeves. First, you want to keep them out of your food. Second, for safety reasons you need to keep long or loose things away from things like blenders or the flame on your stove.

Tropical Smoothie

This treat is extra refreshing on a hot afternoon.

▶ Difficulty: Medium

Makes 2 smoothies

1 cup orange juice
1 banana
½ cup frozen peach slices
½ cup frozen strawberries

1. Put all of the ingredients into a blender.
2. Put the lid on, and blend for 1 minute, or until smooth.

Pour into large glasses and enjoy. For added decoration, garnish the glasses with a slice or two of fresh fruit. It's almost like you're on vacation!

Did You Know...

Food Trivia

Yogurt was first made thousands of years ago by nomadic tribes in West Asia and Eastern Europe.

Just Peachy Smoothie

For peach lovers, there's nothing better than this icy delight.

▶ Difficulty: Medium

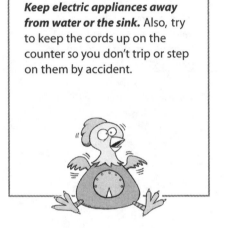

Makes 2 smoothies

About 2 cups vanilla frozen yogurt
    or ice cream
½ cup milk
1 medium fresh peach, peeled, pitted,
    and cut up into chunks (or ½ cup
    frozen peach slices, unsweetened)
1 Tbsp. honey

1. Put all of the ingredients into a blender.
2. Put the lid on, and blend for 1 minute, or until smooth.

Pour into large glasses and enjoy. This drink is best in the summer, when the freshest fruit is available.

Best Banana-Berry Smoothie

You can enjoy this smoothie any time of year. It's delicious, refreshing, and good for you.

▶ Difficulty: Medium

Makes 2 smoothies

1 banana (frozen)
½ cup frozen berries, raspberries,
    blueberries, strawberries, or any
    combination you choose
1 (8-ounce) container vanilla yogurt
½ cup milk

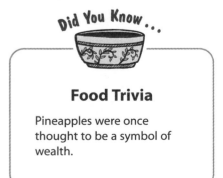

1. Put all of the ingredients into a blender.
2. Put the lid on, and blend for 1 minute, or until smooth.

Pour into large glasses and enjoy.

Grape Ice Delight

You can make these for a special occasion, or just enjoy them anytime yourself.

▶ Difficulty: Easy

Makes 1 delight

2 scoops lemon or lime sherbet
½ cup grape juice
½ cup ginger ale

1. Put the sherbet into a tall glass.
2. Pour the grape juice over the sherbet and then pour the ginger ale over the top.

Did You Know...

Food Trivia

Pineapples were once thought to be a symbol of wealth.

Creamy Dreamy Root Beer Float

Watch the foam appear as you pour the root beer. What a treat!

▶ Difficulty: Easy

Makes 1 float

2 scoops vanilla ice cream or frozen yogurt
1 cup root beer

1. Put the ice cream into a tall glass.
2. Pour the root beer over the top.

Use fun colored straws and iced-tea spoons to get every last delicious drop!

Hot Apple Cider

Hot cider is a wonderful drink to serve at a party, or to sip on a cool, fall night.

▶ Difficulty: Hard

Makes 8 servings

8 cups (½ gallon) apple cider
1 orange, seeded and cut into thin slices
2 cinnamon sticks
6 cloves

1. In a large saucepan, combine the cider, orange wedges, cinnamon, and cloves.
2. Heat just to boiling.
3. Reduce the heat to a simmer and cook, uncovered, for 30 minutes.

Remove the orange slices, cinnamon sticks, and cloves before serving.

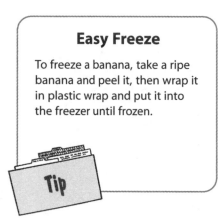

Easy Freeze

To freeze a banana, take a ripe banana and peel it, then wrap it in plastic wrap and put it into the freezer until frozen.

Tip

Healthy Habits

Be sure to wash your hands with soap and water before touching food. It is also important to wash your hands after handling raw meat or fish, before you start touching other things.

Tangy Orange Fizz

This tangy, tasty punch is perfect at a pool party, or after a game of baseball in the yard.

▶ Difficulty: Easy

Makes 6 servings

2 cups lemonade
2 cups orange juice
2 cups sparkling water

 OR

1. In a large pitcher, combine all of the ingredients.
2. Stir well.

Serve over ice. If you make a double batch for a party, pour the tangy orange fizz into a punch bowl with ice on the side (so the punch doesn't get watery).

Party Time Punch

Try adding scoops of orange, lemon, or lime sherbet.

▶ Difficulty: Easy

Makes about 12 servings of punch

1 (12-ounce) can frozen orange
   juice concentrate, thawed
1 (12-ounce) can frozen lemonade concentrate, thawed
1 (2-liter) bottle ginger ale
2 oranges, seeded and cut into thin slices

1. In a large punch bowl, combine all of the ingredients.
2. Mix well, until the concentrates are dissolved.

Serve over ice in a punchbowl, or tall pitcher, and garnish with orange slices.

Food Trivia

Cola was first invented by mixing carbonated water into cough syrup.

Deputy: How tough is that outlaw you just captured?

Sheriff: He's so tough, when he wants a cup of tea, he swallows a teabag and a mouthful of water and sits on the stove till the water boils!

What's Cookin' at Your House?

Are you a creative cook? You may decide to experiment with some of these recipes. If you try something new and everyone likes it, make notes here so you remember what you changed. You can also use this space to write down special recipes from your friends or family.

Recipe Title: ....

Makes .... **servings**

Ingredients:

....

....

....

....

....

Directions:

....

....

....

....

....

....

....

....

....

....

Chapter 9

Let's Play Some More

itchen creations are not all about food. You might be surprised at what you can make using regular ingredients. Things that are safe and pretty harmless will keep your parents happy, but things that are fun will keep you happy!

Is it a rainy day, a slumber party, or even an afternoon with the babysitter? Next time you are looking for something to do, head to the kitchen and try these creative ideas.

Leftovers

Take a word from column B and write it next to a word in column A to make the name of a familiar food. There may be more than one way to match up all the words—just make sure there are no leftovers!

I've got my part!

I have my part, too!

COLUMN A	COLUMN B
CUP_____	FRIES
STRAW_____	MELT
POTATO_____	SAUCE
PEANUT_____	ROLL
POP_____	BURGER
CORN_____	BERRY
COLE_____	CORN
HOT_____	BUTTER
HAM_____	CAKE
FRENCH_____	SALAD
TUNA_____	SLAW
APPLE_____	CHIPS
EGG_____	DOG

Handmade Play Dough

Making play dough on a cold or rainy day can be just the project to keep you busy while having fun with your siblings and friends.

▶ Difficulty: Medium

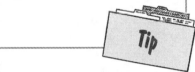

Be Prepared

This play dough may seem softer to you than the kind you buy at the store. It is so easy to squeeze and squish, but may be somewhat more difficult to mold. If you store your dough properly, it should last for a long time.

Tip

Makes 2 cups of dough

2 cups flour
1 cup salt
4 tsp. cream of tartar
1 package unsweetened powdered soft drink mix, any flavor or color, or several drops of food coloring
2 cups water
½ cup oil

1. In large saucepan, combine the flour, salt, cream of tartar, and powdered soft drink mix or food coloring.
2. Add in the water and oil.
3. Heat on stovetop at medium heat and cook mixture, while stirring frequently.
4. As the mixture gets hot, it will turn into a thick dough.
5. When this happens, remove the pan from the stovetop.
6. Let the dough cool down before you dump it out and play with it.

Store your play dough in an airtight container or resealable plastic bag when you are not using it.

Ted: I'm going to get an "F" in cooking class.

Fred: Why?

Ted: The dog keeps eating my homework!

Making Bubbles

Making bubbles is always a blast. If you want to make different colored bubbles, just add a few drops of food coloring to your solution.

▶ Difficulty: Easy

Makes about 1 quart of bubble solution

3 cups water
1 cup Joy brand dishwashing liquid (for some reason this is the brand that works best)
⅓ cup light corn syrup
Bubble wands, any size or shape

1. Mix the water, dishwashing soap, and corn syrup together in an airtight container with a tight cover.
2. Once the solution is mixed well, you can either use it by yourself in the container, or put the solution into a shallow bowl so more people can reach it at once.

Use your bubble wand to blow bubbles of all sizes.

Get Creative

If you don't have an old wand left over from other jars of bubbles, you can make your own out of a wire hanger or a plastic strawberry basket. Experiment with different sizes and shapes, and see what happens!

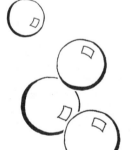

Cereal Necklaces

You can also make these necklaces on regular string, and take them in the car for an enjoyable snack.

▶ Difficulty: Easy

Make as many as you need

1 cup O-shaped cereal (like Cheerios, Froot Loops, or any other brand)
Long, thin licorice strings

1. Depending on what you have around, you can use a few different cereal Os, putting each kind into the separate cups of a muffin tin.
2. Holding onto the licorice string, thread on different Os in different patterns, or colors—or flavors! (Make sure one end of the string is knotted, otherwise your Os will come sliding right off!)
3. Knot the ends together to wear the necklace, or just eat it as is.

This is great for parties because it's not only is it a snack, it's also an activity *and* a party favor!

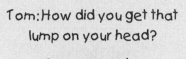

Tom: How did you get that lump on your head?

Tim: I got hit by some beans.

Tom: How could some little beans give you such a big lump?

Tim: They were still in the can!

Play It Safe

Know where to find things, and where to put them away. By keeping everything in its place, you will have a clean cooking area, and you won't lose things.

Edible Finger Paints

This is an easy project for a rainy day. Not only will you enjoy creating, but maybe your parents will take part in the fun, too.

▶ Difficulty: Easy

1 (3.9-ounce package) instant vanilla pudding
2 cups cold water
Food coloring

1. In a large bowl, use a whisk to combine the pudding mix with the cold water.
2. Pour the mixture into a muffin tin pan or several small bowls.
3. Stir several drops of food coloring into each bowl to make different colors.
4. Refrigerate for 10–15 minutes before painting.

Use plain paper or coloring books to show off your creativity, and enjoy your creations!

Good Thinking

Even though this "paint" is edible, remember that lots of hands and fingers have been in it. After painting and playing with the paints, you probably want to limit the amount that goes into your mouth.

edible: Able to be eaten

Graham Cracker Houses

Try these at the holidays to make festive, decorated creations.

▶ Difficulty: Easy

One house of your very own design

4 or more graham cracker rectangles
½ cup peanut butter
Various tubes of decorating icing
Candy shapes like gumballs, gumdrops, chocolate chips,
    Hershey's Kisses, M & M Candies
Cookie decorations like candy sprinkles, stars, and silver balls

1. Place a graham cracker on a flat surface.
2. Spread a thin layer of peanut butter along all four edges.
3. Stand another graham cracker upright on one edge and
    proceed with another graham cracker on another edge.
4. Keep building using your peanut butter as "glue" to create
    the house of your dreams.
5. Add decorating icing, candies, and sprinkles to complete
    your home.

Put your house on display or eat it up!

Snack Attack

If you are planning to snack on your house, do so within a day or two of making it, as the icing and candy will harden and begin to get stale.

Tip

What do frogs eat with their hamburgers?

French flies!

In the Kitchen

Use everything you learned in this book to answer the questions below, and fill them in to the numbered puzzle grid. We left you some T-I-D-B-I-T-S to help!

Cooking is fun! Can I help?

Sure!

Sure!

ACROSS
1. After breakfast you eat _____.
3. All the recipes in this book taste _____!
5. A short name for a long sandwich
7. A crunchy shell filled with spicy meat and cheese
10. Do this to potatoes to make them fluffy.
11. You have to "be a member" to eat this sandwich.
13. To cut a thin piece
14. Pot topper
15. You'll use one of these to flip a flapjack.
17. Important! Do this before you start cooking!
21. Cut that carrot into tiny cubes!
22. It would be great to have one of these to clean the kitchen!
26. Three-sided chips
30. Put something in a microwave and "____" it.
31. Yeast helps bread to ____.
32. Sweet and crunchy oats, seeds, and nuts that are good for breakfast or for snacks.
33. Why was the ice cream lonely? Because the banana _____!

DOWN
1. You can use this in a salad.
2. Cheezy chips
4. Baked 12 at a time in metal cups, they're sooo good, you'll eat them up!
6. Little, tiny vegetables are called "____."
8. Favorite round and chewy breakfast bread
9. Creamy soup that's good with corn or clams
11. A bowl with holes
12. What you find in the center of a cherry or an olive
16. The opposite of "rightunders"
17. You beat eggs and cream with this.
18. What does a gingerbread man put on his bed? Cookie _____!
19. These critters help bread to rise
20. On a hot day, it's good to drink cold lemon____.
23. A thin stream of liquid (or a light rain!)
24. This kind of Italian "pie" is a lunch and dinner favorite.
25. Use a spatula to ____ your flapjacks.
27. Waffle topper
28. Who likes "woofles" for breakfast? The ____!
29. A good thing to fill with ice cream

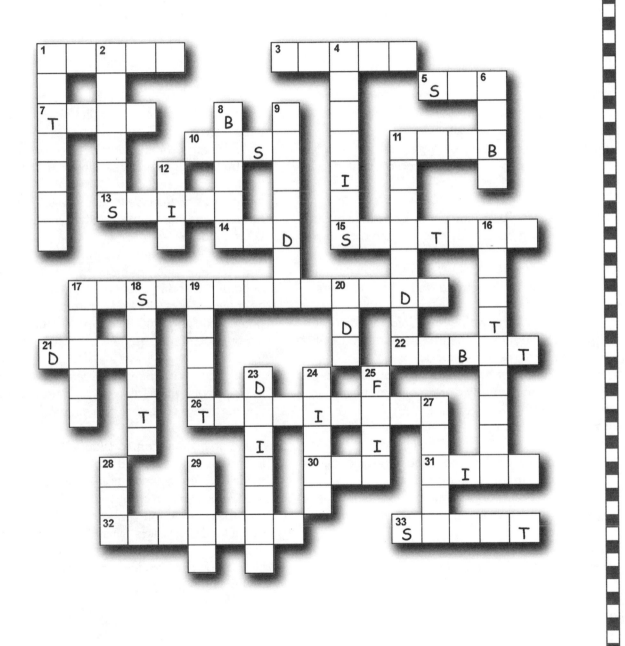

Appendix A

Online Resources

Once you spend some time in the kitchen, you may start looking for more recipe ideas. You may also want information on food, or need a few tips on how to use some of your leftovers. The following Web sites are designed to be family-friendly, so the next time you are planning to cook for your family or company, log on, first, and see what you can discover!

www.burgertown.kidscom.com teaches kids about incorporating beef in the diet through a variety of games and special features.

www.cdc.gov/powerfulbones/ offers good information on ways to stay strong and take good care of your bones.

www.familyfoodzone.com shares information on growing a healthy child through nutrition, family fun, coloring, resources, and more.

www.pork4kids.com helps kids learn about eating pork through a variety of cartoons, features, and recipes.

www.whymilk.com by the creators of the Milk Mustache campaign, teaches kids about the importance of drinking milk and including calcium and dairy foods in their diet.

http://exhibits.pacsci.org/nutrition/ offers fun, games, and activities on nutrition and eating healthy.

http://family.go.com/recipes/kids is part of Disney Online/Family Fun, and offers tips on healthful eating and snacking, food fun, recipes, and ideas for cooking with kids.

http://kidscook.com includes recipes, contests, and cooking kits.

http://kraftfoods.com/html/features/jello.html shares cooking fun and kid fun using Jell-O.

http://nutritionforkids.com teaches children about nutrition and nutritious eating.

http://wheatfoods.org shares information on the importance of wheat in the diet along with a collection of recipes.

www.5aday.org promotes importance of eating five fruits and vegetables a day for better health.

www.ars.usda.gov/is/kids focuses on science, farming, and agricultural activities and information for kids.

www.broccoli.com/mainpage.htm offers information on the nutrition of broccoli through a variety of games, coloring sheets, and recipes.

www.delmonte.com/kids/index.htm uses fun, games, cooking, and coloring to focus on the importance of including fruits and vegetables in the diet.

www.dole5aday.com helps kids learn the importance of eating five fruits and vegetables each day through a variety of games and fun activities.

www.fda.gov/oc/opacom/kids/default.htm offers information, games, and more on food safety, foods and drugs, teen health, and more.

www.idd-inc.com/pyramidtracker/ (directed toward seven- to ten-year-olds) helps kids learn about the Food Guide Pyramid and tracking their dietary intake.

www.kidfood.org helps kids learn about nutrition and eating right.

www.kidscookingcorner.com is a kid-friendly site that includes recipes, cooking secrets, jokes, and an art gallery from kids.

www.kidsfood.com features a collection of cooking tips, resources, and recipes.

Appendix B

Glossary

A lot of the terms in this book were explained in Chapter 1, but others are mixed in with the recipes. Here, all your important terms are listed alphabetically. If you want to know about a word that's not in this list, look in the dictionary, or ask an adult. Understanding cooking terms helps you know what you're doing in the kitchen. It also helps you know what you are getting the next time you eat out.

appetizer—a food or drink that stimulates the appetite and is usually served before a meal

bake—to cook something inside the oven, using the heat from the bottom

baking pan—a square or rectangular pan (glass or metal) used for baking and cooking food in the oven

basting—to moisten at intervals with a liquid (such as melted butter or pan drippings) during cooking

batter—a mixture made from ingredients like sugar, eggs, flour, and water that is used to make cakes, cookies, and pancakes

beat—to mix hard with a spoon, fork, whisk, or electric mixer

blend—to mix foods together until smooth

blender—an electric appliance used for blending liquids and grinding food

boil—to cook in a liquid until bubbles appear or until a liquid reaches its boiling point (water boils at 212° Fahrenheit/100° Celsius). Note: Water cannot get hotter than its boiling point, it can only make steam faster.

broil—to put food under the broiler part of the oven, where the heat source is on top of the food

brown—to cook at low to medium heat until foods turn brown

can opener—a tool, either manual or electric, designed to open cans

casserole dish—a glass dish, usually a 1-quart or 2-quart size, used to make casseroles or baked mixtures in the oven

chill—to refrigerate food until it is cold

chop—to cut food into small pieces with a knife, blender, or food processor

colander—a metal (or sometimes plastic) bowl with holes in it used to drain water or liquid from foods (such as pasta or vegetables)

confectioners' sugar—Finely powdered sugar with cornstarch added

cookie sheet—a flat metal sheet used for baking cookies or other non-runny items

cool—to let the food sit at room temperature until it is no longer hot

craving—a great desire or hunger

cream—to mix ingredients like sugar, butter, and eggs together until they are smooth and creamy

cutting board—a board made from wood or hard plastic used when cutting or chopping ingredients

dice—to chop food into small, square (like dice), even-sized pieces

drain—to pour off a liquid in which the food has been cooked or stored

drizzle—to sprinkle drops of liquid, like chocolate syrup or an icing, lightly over the top of something, like cookies or a cake

dutch oven—a heavy pot with a tight-fitting domed cover

edible—able to be eaten

electric mixer—an electric appliance used for mixing ingredients (like cake batter) together

fold—to gently combine ingredients together from top to bottom until they are just mixed together

garnish—to add colorful, but tasty, "decorations" to a meal

glass measuring cup—a glass cup, used to measure liquids, with various measurements printed along the side

grate—to shred food into tiny pieces with a shredder, blender, or food processor

grease—to rub a baking pan or a dish with butter, margarine, or oil so food cooked on it won't stick (Canned cooking spray will work, too.)

hummus—a Middle Eastern dish that is a mixture of mashed chickpeas, garlic, and other ingredients, used especially as a dip for pita

ice cream scoop—a plastic or metal tool, shaped like a giant spoon, used to scoop ice cream from a carton

knead—to fold, press, and turn dough to make it the right consistency

knives—sharp utensils used for cutting, slicing, or carving (Always be careful when using knives—good ones are very sharp!)

measuring cups—plastic or metal cups in different sizes, used to measure dry ingredients

measuring spoons—plastic or metal spoons in different sizes, used to measure smaller amounts of both liquid and dry ingredients

meat mallet—a tool used to pound, flatten, and tenderize beef, chicken, and other meat

microwave oven—a small oven that cooks food very quickly by cooking with electromagnetic waves (microwaves)

mince—to cut food into very small pieces

mix—to stir two or more ingredients together until they are evenly combined

mixing bowls—bowls (in various sizes) in which you mix ingredients together

molasses—the thick, brown syrup that is separated from raw sugar during the refining process

muffin tins—metal or glass pans with small, round cups used for baking muffins and cupcakes

opaque—cloudy; not clear or transparent

oven—a kitchen appliance for baking or broiling food

oven mitts/pot holders—mittens or pads used to hold hot pots, pans, baking sheets, and plates

pastry brush—a small brush used to spread melted butter or margarine, or sauces over food

pie plate—shallow dish made of glass or metal, used for making pies

pitted—without the center pit (as in peaches, olives, or avocados)

pizza cutter—a tool with a rolling cutter used to easily cut pizzas, dough, or breads

plate—a flat dish used to serve food

potato masher—a tool used to mash cooked potatoes, or anything soft, to make them smooth

preheat—to turn the oven on to the desired temperature and let it heat up before using it for cooking

preserves—Fruit that is canned, or made into jams or jellies for future use

puree—to mix in a blender or food processor until food is smooth and has the consistency of applesauce or a milkshake

rolling pin—a wooden or plastic roller used to flatten items such as dough for a piecrust

rubber spatula—a tool used for removing batter or liquids from the sides of a bowl

saucepan—a pot with a projecting handle used for stovetop cooking

sauté—to cook food on the stovetop in a skillet with a little liquid or oil

simmer—to cook over low heat until the food almost boils

skillet—a pan used for frying, stir-frying, and sautéing food in hot fat or oil

slice—to cut food into even-sized slices

spatula—a flat metal or plastic utensil used to lift, turn, and flip foods like eggs, cookies, and hamburgers

steam—to put food over a pan of boiling water so the steam can cook it

stir—to continuously mix food with a spoon

stir-fry—to cook food on the stovetop in a very hot pan while stirring constantly

stove—a kitchen appliance with gas or electric burners used for cooking food (also called "range")

tortilla—a round, flat, thin cornmeal or wheat flour bread usually eaten with hot topping or filling

vegetable peeler—sometimes called a potato or carrot peeler, used to peel the skin off of fruit or vegetables

whip—to beat rapidly with a whisk, electric mixer, or an eggbeater

whisk—a utensil used for mixing and stirring liquid ingredients, like eggs and milk, together

wooden spoon—a big spoon made out of wood that is used for mixing and stirring just about any kind of food

PUZZLE ANSWERS

page 7 • Bubbles

1. W A (F) F L E
2. P (U) D D I N G
3. N O O (D) L E S
4. E G (G) R O L L
5. F R I (E) S

BONUS: **F U D G E**

page 9 • Measuring Spoon Math

Flour = __32__ Tbsp.

Sugar = __24__ Tbsp.

Cocoa = __4__ Tbsp.

page 16 • A Tasty Puzzle!

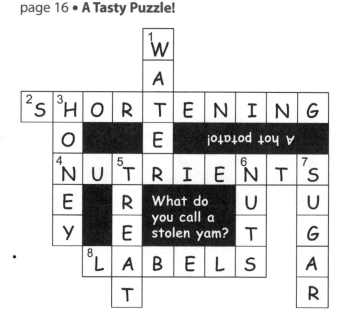

page 18 • Breakfast Scrambles

1. What does a centipede have for breakfast?
   B A C O N AND L E G S

2. What does a lighthouse keeper have for breakfast?
   B E A C O N AND E G G S

3. What does a spook have for breakfast?
   G H O S T   T O A S T

page 22 • **Bagel #1**   Peanut Butter

page 24 • **Bagel #2**   Hummus

page 25 • **Mystery Meal #1**   French Toast

page 26 • **Bagel #3**   Grape Jelly

page 29 • **Bagel #4**   Cream Cheese

page 31 • **Bagel #5**   Egg Salad

page 34 • What's for Lunch?

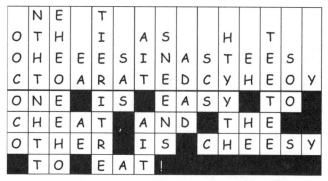

page 42 • **Mystery Meal #2**   Macaroni and Cheese

PUZZLE ANSWERS

page 44 • **Chips and Dip**

page 47 • **Mystery Meal #3**   Garden Salad

page 49 • **The Apple Barrel**   They can make applesauce! Or, if they are in a hurry, they can divide each apple evenly into quarters, and each boy can take one quarter of each apple.

page 50 • **Mystery Meal #4**   Chocolate Chip Cookies

page 53 • **Mystery Meal #5**   Egg Salad Sandwich

page 56 • **The Soup Pot**

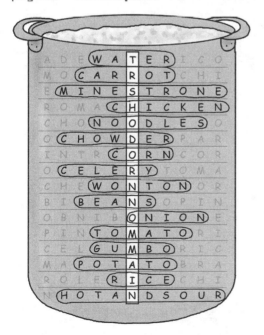

page 64 • **Oodles of Noodles**

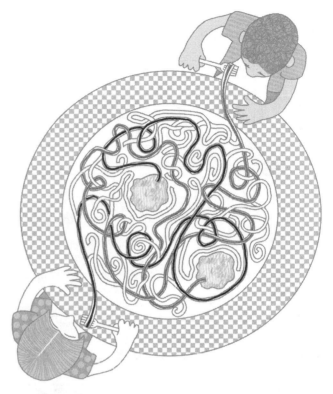

page 92 • **Who's Who?**

PUZZLE ANSWERS

page 98 • **Cut the Cake**

page 107 • **Mystery Meal #6**   Blueberry Muffins

page 110 • **I'm Thirsty**

MILK	Code is a simple number substitution, A=1, B=2, etc.
SODA	Word is turned upside-down and backwards.
SHAKE	Word is represented by a picture of a person shaking.
WATER	H_2O is the chemical formula for water.
JUICE	For each letter in the code, substitute the letter before it in the alphabet.
ICED TEA	Word is represented by a picture of the letter "T" with icicles hanging on it.

page 118 • **Leftovers**

COLUMN A

CUP CAKE

STRAW BERRY

POTATO SALAD

PEANUT BUTTER

POP CORN

CORN CHIPS

COLE SLAW

HOT DOG

HAM BURGER

FRENCH FRIES

TUNA MELT

APPLE SAUCE

EGG ROLL

page 124 • **In the Kitchen**

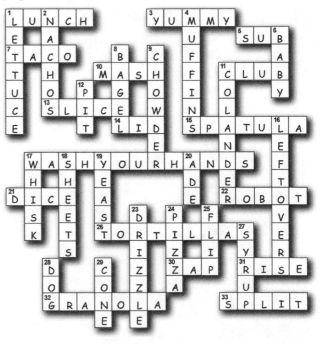

Index

The Everything® KIDS' Series!

Packed with tons of information, activities, and puzzles, the Everything® Kids' books are perennial bestsellers that keep kids active and engaged.

Each book is two-color, 8" x 9¼", and 144 pages.

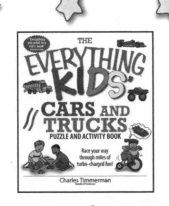

The Everything® Kids' Cars and Trucks Puzzle and Activity Book
1-59337-703-7, $7.95

The Everything® Kids' First Spanish Puzzle and Activity Book
1-59337-717-7, $7.95

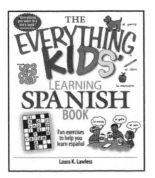

The Everything® Kids' Learning Spanish Book
1-59337-716-9, $7.95

The Everything® Kids' Princess Puzzle and Activity Book
1-59337-704-5, $7.95

Other Everything® Kids' Titles Available

The Everything® Kids' Animal Puzzle & Activity Book
1-59337-305-8

The Everything® Kids' Baseball Book, 4th Ed.
1-59337-614-6

The Everything® Kids' Bible Trivia Book
1-59337-031-8

The Everything® Kids' Bugs Book
1-58062-892-3

The Everything® Kids' Christmas Puzzle & Activity Book
1-58062-965-2

The Everything® Kids' Cookbook
1-58062-658-0

The Everything® Kids' Crazy Puzzles Book
1-59337-361-9

The Everything® Kids' Dinosaurs Book
1-59337-360-0

The Everything® Kids' Halloween Puzzle &
Activity Book
1-58062-959-8

The Everything® Kids' Hidden Pictures Book
1-59337-128-4

The Everything® Kids' Horses Book
1-59337-608-1

The Everything® Kids' Joke Book
1-58062-686-6

The Everything® Kids' Knock Knock Book
1-59337-127-6

The Everything® Kids' Math Puzzles Book
1-58062-773-0

The Everything® Kids' Mazes Book
1-58062-558-4

The Everything® Kids' Money Book
1-58062-685-8

The Everything® Kids' Nature Book
1-58062-684-X

The Everything® Kids' Pirates Puzzle and Activity Book
1-59337-607-3

The Everything® Kids' Puzzle Book
1-58062-687-4

The Everything® Kids' Riddles & Brain Teasers Book
1-59337-036-9

The Everything® Kids' Science Experiments Book
1-58062-557-6

The Everything® Kids' Sharks Book
1-59337-304-X

The Everything® Kids' Soccer Book
1-58062-642-4

The Everything® Kids' Travel Activity Book
1-58062-641-6

All titles are $6.95 or $7.95 unless otherwise noted.

Available wherever books are sold!
To order, call 800-258-0929, or visit us at *www.adamsmedia.com*
Everything® and everything.com® are registered trademarks of F+W Publications, Inc.
Prices subject to change without notice.

A silly, goofy, and undeniably icky addition to
the Everything® Kids' series . . .

The Everything® Kids'
GROSS
Series

Chock–full of sickening entertainment for hours of disgusting fun.

The Everything® Kids'
Gross Jokes Book
1-59337-448-8, $7.95

The Everything® Kids' Gross
Puzzle & Activity Book
1-59337-447-X, $7.95

The Everything® Kids'
Gross Mazes Book
1-59337-616-2, $7.95

The Everything® Kids' Gross
Hidden Pictures Book
1-59337-615-4, $7.95